CULTURES OF THE WORLD™

MYANMAR

Saw Myat Yin

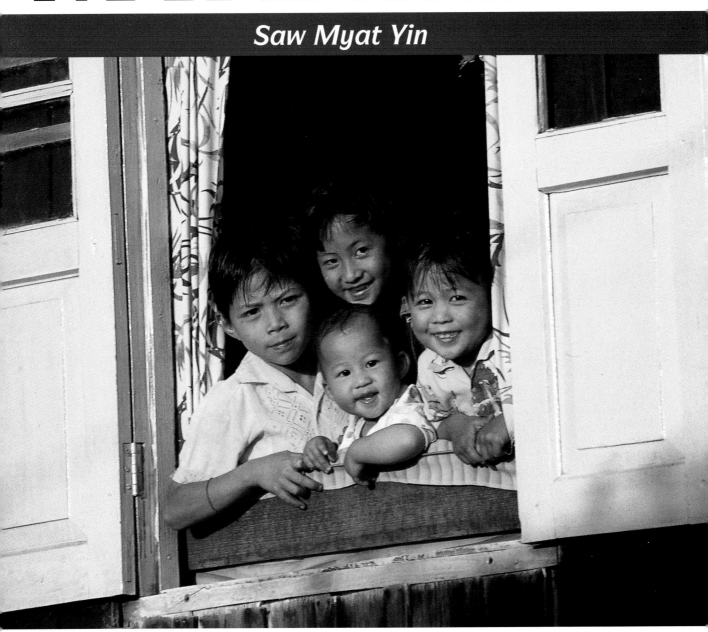

BENCHMARK BOOKS

MARSHALL CAVENDISH
NEW YORK

PICTURE CREDITS
Jon Burbank, Bes Stock, Steve Bly, Birgitte Dessau,
Jean-Leo Dugast, Alain Evrard, Michael Freeman, G.A.
Grinsted, Hans Hayden, Peter Korn, Noazesh Ahmed,
Julia Oh, Harold Pfeiffer, Photobank, Luca I. Tettoni,
Paul Tracey, Veronique Sanson, Bill Wassaman, Diane
Wilson, Alison Wright

ACKNOWLEDGMENTS
Thanks to Jai Kasturi, Middle Eastern and Asian
Languages and Cultures Department, Columbia
University, for his expert reading of this manuscript

PRECEDING PAGE:
Myanmar children smile happily from their home.

Marshall Cavendish Corporation
99 White Plains Road
Tarrytown, NY 10591
Website: www.marshallcavendish.com

© 1990, 2002 by Times Media Private Limited
All rights reserved. First edition 1990
Second edition 2002

Originated and designed by
Times Books International, an imprint of
Times Media Private Limited, a member of the
Times Publishing Group

Printed in Malaysia

Library of Congress Cataloging-in-Publication Data:
Yin, Saw Myat, 1946-
    Myanmar / Saw Myat Yin.
        p. cm. — (Cultures of the world)
    Includes bibliographical references and index.
    ISBN 0-7614-1353-7
    1. Burma—Juvenile literature. [1. Burma] I. Title. II.
Series.

DS527.4 .Y564 2001
959.1—dc21   2001025412
6 5 4 3 2

CONTENTS

**An old Kayin couple
enjoying a smoke.**

A procession of women carrying offerings to a Buddhist initiation ceremony. Contrary to the Western image of Asian women as passive, Myanmar women are independent and active outside the home. Bazaars are almost entirely run by women who seem to have a flair for business.

INTRODUCTION

MYANMAR, or the Union of Myanmar as it is now officially named, is a country little known to the rest of the world, even to its Asian neighbors. For more than a quarter century, it has been so isolated it seems to have almost disappeared from the map of the world.

People who have heard of Myanmar know it as "the land of pagodas." Yet there is more to Myanmar than that. Its cultural life is a rich and unique mix of Buddhist teachings and elements of Hindu culture. The Myanmar, regardless of whether they are country folk or urbanites, are a warm and friendly people who always have time to sit and exchange tales or the latest jokes over a cup of tea.

This book, part of the series *Cultures of the World*, explores this little-known country where the lifestyle of the people reflects a special blend of tradition and modernity.

GEOGRAPHY

MYANMAR IS A LAND of contrasts in landscapes, with snowy mountains in the far north and sunny, tropical beaches in the south.

GEOGRAPHICAL LOCATION

Myanmar lies in mainland Southeast Asia, bordered by India in the northwest, Bangladesh and the Bay of Bengal in the west, the Andaman Sea in the southwest, China in the north, and Laos and Thailand in the east.

Apart from a 1,400-mile-long (2,252-km) coastline, Myanmar is surrounded by a horseshoe-shaped ring of mountains that forms a natural border of almost 4,000 miles (6,436 km) with its neighbors. The main rivers are the Ayeyarwady, Chindwin, Thanlwin, and Sittaung. The country, about the size of the state of Texas, covers 261,228 square miles (676,580 sqaure km) and consists of the seven states of Rakhine, Chin, Kachin, Kayin (or Karen), Kayah, Shan, and Mon.

SEASONS

Myanmar has three seasons: the rainy season (monsoon) from July to October, a cool season from November to February, and a hot season from March to June. Rainfall is as much as 200 inches (508 cm) a year in the coastal regions, 100 inches (254 cm) in the plains, and an average of 29 inches (74 cm) in the central part. Temperatures reach 113°F (45°C) in central Myanmar, and fall to 32°F (0°C) in the north. The average annual temperature varies from 71°F (22°C) in the highlands of the Shan plateau to 81°F (27°C) in the southern lowlands.

Above: **Myanmar is still largely rural, with many Myanmar living in villages surrounded by rolling green hills and rice fields. There are 65,000 villages in Myanmar.**

Opposite: **Morning light on the Ayeyarwady River.**

7

The Rakhine Yoma, or "Rakhine main range," in the distance, is part of the western ranges and separates the Rakhine coastal strip from the central plain.

Myanmar can be roughly divided into four regions: the northern and western mountainous region, the eastern Shan plateau, the central belt, and the long southern "tail." The region north of Mandalay is commonly referred to as Upper Myanmar, while Yangon and the Ayeyarwady delta are known as Lower Myanmar.

NORTHERN AND WESTERN REGIONS

The northern and western mountains extend from the extreme north down to the western side of Myanmar. The Kachin, Chin, and Rakhine states are located in this region. Some of Burma's highest peaks are here: Mount Hkakabo Razi (19,296 feet/588 m), the highest in Southeast Asia, and Mount Gamlan Razi, both in the extreme north and part of the Kachin range; and Mount Sarameti and Mount Victoria in the Chin range.

Rakhine State in the west has a coastal strip that is wide in the north and narrows toward the south. The resort beaches are located here. Offshore, numerous islands dot the Bay of Bengal and the Andaman Sea.

The vegetation in this region varies from tropical and subtropical to the temperate and alpine forests. There is an abundance of rhododendron, magnolia, juniper, pine, birch, and cherry trees here. Bamboo forests cover a large area of the Rakhine range; wild animals still survive here in the mountains—bears, civet cats, elephants, leopards, and tigers, to name a few. The rare takin, red panda, tapir, snow leopard, and musk deer are found in the northern temperate forests, although some of these animals have been hunted to near extinction.

The capitals of the states of Kachin, Chin, and Rakhine are Myitkyina, Falam, and Sittway, respectively. Near Myitkyina, the tributaries Maykha and Malikha join to form the Ayeyarwady River.

Coconut palms favor the sandy soil of the Rakhine coast.

The rich plains of the central region are the rice bowl of Myanmar, with acres and acres of land devoted to rice-planting.

CENTRAL REGION

The central region has a dry zone, but here are also the rich river valleys and plains of the mighty Ayeyarwady, the Chindwin—a tributary of the Ayeyarwady—and the Sittaung rivers. Low mountain ranges flank many of the river valleys.

In the dry zone, the flora consists of thorny trees and shrubs and cacti. Snakes, especially poisonous vipers, are particularly common here. Petroleum and gas are found in the central region, and agricultural products such as beans, pulses, cotton, onions, chili, oilseeds, and tobacco are also produced here.

Teak and other hardwoods cover the slopes of the mountain ranges, while in the river valleys and plains, the main crop is rice. Jute and sugar cane, important industrial raw materials, are also grown here. Fish and shrimp are bred in ponds and harvested from rivers and creeks.

The main cities in this area are: Yangon (or Rangoon), the capital; Pathein; and Bago, the ancient Mon capital, which is about 45 miles (72 km) north of Yangon. Pyi and Toungoo are also historical capitals. Ancient pagodas and ruins of older habitation can still be seen in these cities today. Other important cities in the dry central region are Mandalay, Monywa, Magway, and Pakokku.

MYANMAR'S LIFELINE

The Ayeyarwady, Myanmar's lifeline, is 1,350 miles (2,172 km) long. Its source is in the Himalayas, and it flows down the middle of Myanmar to the Andaman Sea. It divides Myanmar; most of the towns are on the east bank. The country's historical capitals are also on this side, capitals such as Mandalay, Innwa, Amarapura, Pyi (or Pyay), and Bagan. Only one bridge, the Innwa bridge near Mandalay, spanned the Ayeyarwady until the 1990s. All other crossings are made by boats of all sizes and shapes, from large car ferries to narrow, long rowboats.

The Ayeyarwady is the backbone of the country's transportation system. On this great river one can see steamers carrying passengers and cargo, barges on which families spend their entire lives carrying products up and down the river, and great rafts of bamboo or teak floating down to Yangon for export.

The delta in the south, where the river divides into eight main branches before flowing into the Andaman Sea, is Myanmar's "rice bowl." It is estimated that 60 to 70 percent of rice production comes from this area. This is because the soil here remains fertile from annual flooding and alluvial deposits, and the terrain is most suitable for rice cultivation. The delta covers 13,000 square miles (33,679 square km) and is a veritable network of streams and creeks. The delta area is famous for fish and shrimp and products derived from them.

SHAN PLATEAU

The Shan plateau in eastern Myanmar is a tableland about 3,000 feet (914 m) above sea level that forms the border with China, Laos, and Thailand. The Thanlwin River, Myanmar's longest at 1,749 miles (2,814 km), rises in Tibet and flows down the plateau through narrow gorges. The Shan State is in the northern part of the plateau, and Kayah State is in the southern part. The climate on the plateau is cool all year round.

Pine and cherry trees grow wild here, as do many wild orchids found on trees and rocky clefts; the blue vanda orchid is a native of the Shan plateau.

Tea, fruit such as avocados, pears, oranges, tangerines, and strawberries, and vegetables such as carrots, cabbages, kohlrabi, beans, and peas are cultivated here. Opium is grown in the part of the Shan State that is included in the Golden Triangle, an area where poppies are grown. The majority of the people who live in this part of the Shah State have been fighting a protracted war with the central government for autonomy.

Mogok, in western Shan State, is famous for its rubies, sapphires, and other gems. Lead, silver, tin, tungsten, and marble are also obtained from this area.

TANINTHARYI COASTAL STRIP

The Tanintharyi coastal strip that includes the states of Mon and Tanintharyi is the long "tail" of Myanmar that extends from the Shan plateau down to the isthmus of Kra in the south. The mountain ranges in the east form a natural border with Thailand. Tin and tungsten are mined in this region, and forests are logged.

The only available agricultural land here is a narrow strip between the mountains and the sea. The land is well-used, with rice the main crop. Numerous orchards grow tropical fruit such as pineapple, durian, rambutan, mangosteen, cashew nut, and coconut. Rubber is also grown here.

Offshore fishing and related industries such as canning and preserving are found in the towns of Dawei and Myeik. The Tanintharyi coast has a number of resort beaches, but these are not accessible to foreigners.

The capitals of Mon State and Tanintharyi—Mawlamyine and Dawei, respectively—are trading centers for goods from neighboring Thailand.

THE MYEIK ARCHIPELAGO The Myeik archipelago is a group of about 800 islands off the Tanintharyi coast opposite the town of Myeik. The Salon people who live here are known as sea gypsies and are famous for deep-sea diving for pearls and abalone. They were once feared as pirates of the Andaman Sea.

A "bus" in Mawlamyine, the capital of Mon State. Myanmar ingenuity went to work to convert an old truck into a "bus," using the hardy teakwood that is plentiful in Myanmar.

13

TRANSPORTATION

Myanmar's roads and railways follow the north to south physical arrangement of rivers and mountain ranges. The few east-to-west roads cross mountain ranges. Many rivers also impede road travel.

The roads and railways are a heritage from the British colonizers, and further development has been slow due to economic stagnation and the political isolation, that has barred international aid.

Rivers are important for trade and transportation, especially the Ayeyarwady and Sittaung rivers and their tributaries in the delta. River craft are mostly crowded, old private steamers. The northern portion of the Sittaung and Thanlwin rivers are not navigable, but these rivers are useful as chutes for floating down teak, other hardwoods, and bamboo that have been extracted from the forests.

Air transportation has deteriorated because of a lack of foreign exchange needed for new planes and spare parts. However, in 1993, a new airline, Myanmar Airways International, was incorporated as a joint venture between Myanmar, Singapore, and Brunei.

In the villages bullock carts are still used as a means of transportation, while in the cities, "pickup" trucks with a roof over the body and benches installed serve to supplement bus services run by the government. These vehicles are imported by Myanmar who have gone abroad to study or work (see opposite page, extreme right).

CITIES

Many place names in Myanmar were anglicized by the British when they occupied the country in the 19th century. The present government has restored the Myanmar names to most of the towns and cities.

YANGON Rangoon, renamed its Burmese name Yangon in 1989, is Myanmar's capital and main port. Founded in 1755 by King Alaungpaya, it grew into a trading port after the British annexed lower Burma in 1826. It became the capital after all of Burma fell to the British in 1886.

Yangon, accessible to foreigners only by sea or air, is a quiet, green city with two large lakes. Most high-rise buildings have been built since the 1998 demonstrations; the tallest building is about 20 stories high. Ministries, directorates, and head offices of government organizations are located in Yangon as are institutions of higher learning. The

On a Yangon road one finds old cars, tall, shady roadside trees, and no traffic jams.

THE SHWE DAGON

The Shwe Dagon, on Singuttara Hill in Yangon, is Myanmar's most sacred pagoda. It enshrines Buddha's hair and other holy relics. Originally only 27 feet (8 m) high, it is now 326 feet (99m) in height through successive renovations and additions made by kings and queens.

Gold and precious gems adorn the pagoda and are also buried in the main treasure chamber under the spire. Four staircases (each with about 130 steps) lead to the pagoda, which is surrounded by numerous smaller spires and monasteries. The main platform and surrounding terraces are always full of worshipers who are meditating or praying, and offering flowers, food, candles, and water.

population—including that of the satellite towns of North and South Okkalapa, Thaketa, and the new towns of North and South Dagon—was over 4 million in the late 1990s, with ethnic Myanmar being the majority.

Mandalay is also described as the religious heart of Myanmar, and here many craftsmen ply trades that are related to religion. Workshops turn out all kinds of religious objects and pagoda ornaments, including umbrellas, which are offered to Buddha images or venerated monks as a special honor.

MANDALAY Mandalay is Myanmar's second largest city and main cultural center. It lies on the east bank of the Ayeyarwady, about 500 miles (805 km) north of Yangon. Established in 1857 by King Mindon, it was Myanmar's last capital before it came under British rule. The magnificent Mandalay palace was burned down during World War II. A replica was rebuilt in the 1990s on the palace grounds, which are surrounded by a moat. Many ancient pagodas and monasteries still stand in Mandalay.

Mandalay is famous not only for being a center of Buddhist learning and fine arts, but also for its gold and silver crafts, carving, and weaving. It has a population of 750,000 and is a trading center for agricultural and other products from all parts of Upper Myanmar.

MAWLAMYINE Formerly Moulmein, Mawlamyine is the third largest city and is situated at the mouth of the Thanlwin. It is an important port and trading center for both products of the Tanintharyi area and those that arrive overland from neighboring countries. Mawlamyine is famous for its fruit, and the women usually possess great culinary skill.

PATHEIN Pathein, or Bassein, is Myanmar's second largest port. It is 28 miles (45 km) from the sea on the Pathein River. It has a population of more than 150,000 and is famous for rice, fish, and shrimp, their derived products, and colorful hand-painted umbrellas.

BAGAN

Bagan is situated on the east bank of the Ayeyarwady, about 120 miles (193 km) south of Mandalay. Its 16 square miles (41 square km) are covered by countless pagodas and temples, which date from the 11th century onward; some are in ruins and some stand in gilded splendor.

Bagan was first established as a walled city in A.D. 849. Beginning with King Anawrahta's reign in 1044, Bagan became a powerful kingdom stretching to Bamaw in the north, Thanlwin in the east, Assam, Rakhine, and the Chin hills in the west, and the Mon kingdom in the south. Anawrahta conquered the Mon people and brought to Bagan the king and royal family, artisans, craftspeople, and Theravada Buddhism, which flourished under successive kings who built many pagodas. The architecture, frescoes, murals, plaster carvings, and bas-reliefs of these pagodas have been described as marvelous relics of Bagan's glory. Bagan fell to the Mongols in 1287, and most of the temples are said to have been pulled down by the Myanmar in an attempt to fortify themselves. Bagan's dry climate, probably resulting from excessive felling of trees for firewood to feed brick kilns where pagoda bricks were made, has helped to preserve these precious monuments.

Many pagodas were destroyed by an earthquake in 1975, but international agencies have helped in restoration work. The villagers who once lived in Bagan have been relocated, and the entire area has been closed to settlements.

HISTORY

THE AYEYARWADY VALLEY was inhabited some 5,000 years ago by the Anyathians, hunters and gatherers who used stone and wood tools. Farther north in the eastern part of the Shan State, cave paintings, and stone tools show that there were other early settlers here. The Anyathians and the Shan cave people stayed far from the sea. The earliest settlers on the coast were the Negritos who had come from Indonesia.

ARRIVAL OF THE FIRST BAMARS

A few centuries before Christ, the Mons entered Myanmar from the region that is now Thailand and Cambodia, and settled around the mouths of the Thanlwin and Sittaung rivers. They cultivated and exported rice as well as teak, minerals, and ivory to India, Arabia, China, and Indochina.

At about the same time, some Tibeto-Myanmar tribes, including the Pyus and their allied tribes, left their homeland on the southeastern slopes of the Tibetan plateau and migrated south, entering the upper Ayeyarwady valley. The Pyus, a loosely knit group of tribes who disappeared in the eighth century, were the first migrants to found a great kingdom, at Pyi. The Pyus were a graceful people who were devout Theravada Buddhists. Some centuries later, the Pyus were pushed back by the Mons. In the process, the Bamars (known as Burmans, anthropologically), a people hitherto subject to the Pyus, rose to prominence.

In the 12th century A.D., the Shans, also known as Tais, arrived from Yunnan, northeast of Myanmar. The Bamars of today are descendants of the Mons, the Bamars, the Pyus, and the Shans.

Above: **A burial urn from the prehistoric period, found in Sri Kshetra, Upper Burma.**

Opposite: **An old brick structure of Dhammayangyi Pahto, found in Bagan.**

An 11th-century terra-cotta plaque tells a story about the Buddha before his enlightenment.

FIRST BAMAR EMPIRE (1044–1287)

After the Pyus were pushed north by the Mons, the Bamars established a small settlement of their own and founded the city of Bagan in A.D. 847. After many dynastic struggles during the first two centuries of Bagan's existence, Anawrahta, a Bamar military leader, became king of Bagan in A.D. 1044. During his 33 years as ruler, he conquered the Mons, brought Buddhism to Bagan, and united all of modern Myanmar except for the Shan plateau and parts of Rakhine and Tanintharyi. His reign was known as the First Myanmar Empire and marked the beginning of Myanmar as a distinct political entity. The kingdom survived until 1287, when it fell before the armies of Kublai Khan. For the next three centuries, disunity characterized Myanmar, which had disintegrated into small states.

Taking advantage of the ensuing turmoil after the fall of the First Bamars Empire, the Mons moved south and founded a new kingdom in Bago in Lower Myanmar. The Shans also broke away and extended their territory westward, establishing a capital in Innwa on the banks of the Ayeyarwady. The remaining Bamars withdrew to Toungoo on the Sittaung River to await an opportunity to initiate the reunification of Myanmar, which did not happen for another 260 years.

The First Bamar Empire was established by King Anawrahta after many wars, marking the beginning of Myanmar as a distinct political entity.

SECOND BAMAR EMPIRE (1551–1752)

In 1541 the Bamars under (reigned 1531–1551) took advantage of the frequent wars between the Shans and Mons and captured Innwa and Bago. After his death, however, the kingdom again fell apart.

King Tabinshwehti's brother-in-law and successor, King Bayinnaung (reigned 1551–1581), later reconquered all the lost territory, won Chiang Mai and Ayuthia from the Siamese, and took back Tanintharyi, thus founding the Second Bamar Empire. Other states on the Myanmar-Chinese border and Manipur, now part of India, paid tribute to Myanmar.

During this period, trade with neighboring countries developed; Bago became an important port for traders traveling to China via the Ayeyarwady and northern Myanmar. It was also a convenient stop for traders going to other parts of Southeast Asia by way of Thanlyin, Mottama, and Pathein, which were important ports in Lower Burma.

Foreigners, especially Arabs and Portuguese, were very active in east-west trade. The British, French, and Dutch trading companies were established in Burma in the 17th century when the capital was moved from Bago to Innwa. During the 18th century, the Shans became weaker, and the Mons, with help from the French, captured Innwa in 1752.

THIRD BAMAR EMPIRE (1752–1885)

After conquering Innwa, the Mons tried to control all Myanmar until the Bamar headman of a tiny Shwebo village tract, Alaungpaya, defeated them. After eight years of war, King Alaungpaya was able to unite the country again and founded the Konbaung dynasty, the third and last Bamar empire. He also moved the capital to Innwa.

Hsinbyushin, Alaungpaya's son and successor, invaded Siam (present-day Thailand) and destroyed Ayuthia in 1767. As a result, Tanintharyi was again under Myanmar control. This victory brought to Myanmar Siamese dancers, musicians, and artisans who influenced Myanmar art and literature.

Another development during this time was the conquest of Rakhine by Hsinbyushin's brother, Bodawpaya. During his reign, Bodawpaya improved the tax collection, communications, legal, and educational systems.

During this dynasty, with few exceptions, the death of a king was followed by assassinations and rebellions. The lack of a system for appointing a successor to the throne was one of the reasons for the disunity among the Bamars that resulted in the eventual fall of the Third Bamar Empire.

The Mandalay court of the last Myanmar king, King Thibaw. Founded by King Mindon, Mandalay was formally inaugurated as the capital in 1859.

King Thibaw fought the third and last war with the British and lost. He was exiled to India, his dominions claimed by the victors.

BRITISH RULE (1886–1942)

In 1886, after three wars with the British, Burma became a British colony. The three Anglo-Myanmar wars in 1824–1826, 1852, and 1885 had their origin in British economic and political interests in Burma.

After the first war, Burma lost Rakhine and Tanintharyi. In 1852 the British annexed Lower Burma in order to close the gap between Calcutta and Singapore, and they made it a province of British India. In 1885 Burma tried to make contact with the outside world, especially France, during the reign of the last king, Thibaw. The British, fearing French interference and wanting a monopoly in teak, used a dispute between Burma and a British timber firm, accused of illegal logging, as an excuse to march to Mandalay, the capital at that time. In 1886 all of Burma became a province of British India, and the royal family was exiled to India.

The British introduced the classic divide-and-rule principle, giving the minority states permission to be ruled by their own leaders. They did not recruit ethnic Myanmar for their army. All important posts in the civil service were filled by Indians or other foreigners. Burma's natural resources were exploited by foreigners and profits channeled out of the country. The British allowed Indians to migrate to Burma to alleviate labor shortages in the rice fields. All these factors inspired the Myanmar nationalists to rebel against the British.

In the early 20th century, the nationalist movement, under the leadership of the Young Men's Buddhist Association (YMBA) and Rangoon University student leaders, grew in strength. During World War II, General Aung San led the struggle against the British and the Japanese who occupied the country during the war. After the war the British finally gave Burma its independence.

This 19th-century print shows British soldiers in the Shwe Dagon. Note that the soldiers are wearing army boots. According to Myanmar etiquette, footwear must be removed before entering temple grounds.

GENERAL AUNG SAN

General Aung San is Burma's national hero and the father of Burma's independence. He started his political career as a young student leader at Rangoon University, founding the Thakin movement together with other students. The members of this movement, dissatisfied with having to address the British as *thakin* (master)—feeling that this demeaned the Myanmar people—termed themselves *thakin* and wore traditional Myanmar clothes.

During World War II, General Aung San formed the Thirty Comrades, a group of 30 young men who swore a blood oath. They secretly went to Japan to ask for help and training to remove the British from Burma. The Japanese, however, proved to be ruthless when they came to Burma. Towards the end of World War II, Aung San and his Myanmar Independence Army (BIA) sought the help of the British to drive out the Japanese.

After the war, General Aung San continued to negotiate for independence, which was won on January 4, 1948. Sadly, he did not live to see the day. At On July 19, 1947, General Aung San was assassinated, together with six cabinet ministers, at the age of 32.

General Ne Win meets with peasants at a seminar. General Ne Win, one of General Aung San's Thirty Comrades, came into power in 1962 following a coup. Under him, the government embarked on a policy of isolation, self-reliance, and strict neutrality in world politics. He retired in 1981 but remained in power as chairman of the Burma Socialist Programme Party (BSPP) until 1988.

AFTER INDEPENDENCE

After independence the country remained unsettled with rebellions from the minorities who wanted their own autonomous states and the Communists who had chosen to go underground. Indeed, these insurrections continue to the present day—more than 50 years after independence.

Elections that should have been held soon after independence in 1948 were held three years later, after the army had managed to contain the rioting and regain control of the country. In the 1951 election, the Anti-Fascist People's Freedom League (AFPFL) won. This political party was an offshoot of the Anti-Fascist Organization, a secret party formed during the Japanese occupation.

The political unrest continued to plague the new government. Economic development plans were implemented but without much success. Export earnings fell due to the decline of rice exports, and domestic revenue collection was hampered.

In the late 1950s, with the economy floundering, the AFPFL split into two groups—the "Clean" and the "Stable." As a result of armed clashes in the villages, a caretaker government, consisting of members of the armed forces, was asked to take over in 1958. During the two years of this government, the economy improved and government departments became more efficient.

Elections were held in 1960 to return the country to civil rule. The "Clean" AFPFL, renamed the Pyidaungsu Party, won. The insurrection problem, however, became more severe since the Shans favored secession.

On March 2, 1962, the army once more stepped in and took over the government in a coup d'état. Known as the Revolutionary Government, its highest body was the Revolutionary Council, composed of 17 high-ranking members of the armed forces. The government declared its socialist aims and abolished democracy. The country embarked on a policy of withdrawal and isolation, a self-sufficient economy, and strict neutrality in world politics.

Soon after the revolutionary government came to power, widespread nationalization of trading organizations, banks, industries, schools, and hospitals took place. Many foreigners were obliged to leave.

In 1974 a new constitution was adopted after a national referendum. The country became known as the Socialist Republic of the Union of Burma, and the Burma Socialist Programme Party (BSPP) was the only political party allowed.

In 1988, student-led demonstrations were suppressed by the military which seized power in a coup d'état. The new government, formed by the State Law and Order Restoration Council (SLORC), initially changed the official name of the country to the Union of Burma, and in 1989 to the Union of Myanmar. It declared that the country was no longer on the socialist path. Efforts were made by the SLORC to actively seek foreign investments to modernize industries and build infrastructure projects. In addition, the economy was opened to private entrepreneurs in the 1990s.

Luyechun are welcomed by the local working people. In 1964, the Ministry of Education began the *luyechun* program in which promising young people, selected among students in schools, colleges, and universities, were nurtured for future leadership.

GOVERNMENT

MYANMAR IS AT PRESENT ruled by a military government that came to power after a coup d'état on September 18, 1988.

Prior to 1988, the country had a one-party socialist government. The Burma Socialist Programme Party (BSPP) had based its policies on "The Myanmar Way to Socialism," a program of socialism and Buddhism, declared on April 30, 1962. In 1974 a new constitution was adopted and a new flag and state seal were introduced.

The government consisted of the *Pyithu Hluttaw*, the parliament, with the Council of State and four subordinate organs of state power: the Council of Ministers, the Council of People's Justices, the Council of People's Attorneys, and the Council of People's Inspectors. The Council of State was elected by the parliament; the chairman of the Council of State was also the president of the Socialist Republic of the Union of Burma.

Left: **The Rangoon City Hall.**

Opposite: **The Victoria High Court in Yangon.**

29

Students—some masked for protection, some bearing flags—take to the streets to demand democracy during the 1998 demonstrations.

POLITICAL UPHEAVAL

A series of political events throughout 1988 caused an upheaval in the country's government. The chief reason for political unrest was the impoverished state of the country caused by years of economic mismanagement, a prolonged insurgency problem, and a heavy foreign debt. Beginning with student demonstrations, originating from a tea-shop brawl in the capital in early 1987, the revolt spread to include the general population in Rangoon, Mandalay, and other cities. The demonstrations became anarchic and violent throughout the months of July, August, and September 1988. The unrest was brutally suppressed, and finally resulted in a coup d'état on September 18, 1988. Martial law was imposed immediately after the coup and was not lifted until mid-1991.

The State Law and Order Restoration Council (SLORC), with local governing bodies called State Law and Order Restoration Committees at the state, division, township, sector, and ward levels, changed its name to the State Peace and Development Council (SPDC) in 1990.

THE UNION OF MYANMAR

Soon after the coup, the country was renamed the Union of Burma which was later changed to the Union of Myanmar. Names of certain towns were also changed to their equivalents in the Myanmar langauge. Rangoon, the capital, was renamed Yangon.

The military government held the promised elections in May 1990. These were the first elections held since 1960. A large number of political parties (over 200) registered with the General Elections Commission. The largest party, the National League for Democracy (NLD), was headed by Daw Aung San Suu Kyi, the daughter of General Aung San. Although she was placed under house arrest in 1989, the NLD won the elections in a landslide victory. However, the SLORC/SPDC has yet to hand over powers to NLD, and Aung San Suu Kyi remained under house arrest until 1996. In 1991, she was awarded the Nobel Peace Prize. She has received numerous other prizes over the years.

A National Convention, made up of various people from the councils of state power, has been drawing up a new constitution in which the military is expected to be given a major role in the running of the country.

Daw Aung San Suu Kyi, daughter of national hero General Aung San, came home to Myanmar in April 1988 to nurse her ailing mother but soon became involved in politics.

ECONOMY

MYANMAR IS A LARGELY rural country with more than 70 percent of the population living in rural areas and over two-thirds of the population dependent on agriculture for a living. Of the labor force of 16.5 million, between 62 to 68 percent are estimated to be in agriculture. Nearly half of the gross domestic product (a measure of a country's production) comes from the primary sector, including agriculture, forestry, fishing, and livestock-rearing. About 25 million acres (10 million hectares) of land are cultivated out of a total of 45.5 million acres (18.4 million hectares) of usable land; about 12.6 million acres (5.1 million hectares) are rice fields.

FARMING

Unlike in the West, in Myanmar farmers do not live on individual farms but in villages surrounded by fields. There are over 14,000 village tracts in Myanmar. The farmers go out to the fields every day where there usually are small huts for resting and eating. Although technically all land is owned by the state, farmers own the land they work for all practical purposes.

The main areas for rice growing are the Ayeyarwady delta, the coastal regions of Rakhine and Tanintharyi, and the Sittaung valley. Other areas also grow rice, but only for local consumption. Beans, pulses (seeds of leguminous plants), and oil seed are cultivated in the dry regions in central Myanmar and toward the northwest. Onions, chilis, and tobacco are also grown here.

The hill peoples cultivate many kinds of crops, but only for their own consumption and for barter because the terrain makes agriculture possible only on a limited scale.

Opium cultivation is said to form a substantial part of cash crop cultivation in the Shan State, but efforts are being made to encourage other types of cash crops such as tea, coffee, and sunflowers.

OTHER OCCUPATIONS

Apart from agriculture, the Myanmar engage in trading, manufacturing, and services. Such occupations are found mainly in the urban centers. In 1998, 9.7 percent of the labor force was in wholesale and retail trade, 9.07 percent in manufacturing, 2.18 percent in construction, and the rest in other sectors such as mining, construction, transportation, and communications. In 1999 the gross domestic product (GDP) was composed of agriculture (34.3%), manufacturing and mining (11%), trade (20.9%), services (18.8%), and others (15%).

Jade is smuggled from Myanmar into neighboring countries, as are antiques and other precious resources, in exchange for manufactured goods that are in short supply in Myanmar.

INFORMAL TRADE

The informal trade sector, or the "black market," has been a large part of the economy since the years of socialism. Black marketeering is a result of poor quality or the lack of local consumer items. Goods have been flowing in from Myanmar's neighboring countries in exchange for Myanmar's precious resources such as forest products, livestock, gems and minerals, agricultural products, and antiques. These were exchanged for common plastic household items, medicine, clothing and textiles, and food and beverages. Although the economy is more open now, informal trade continues.

INDUSTRIES

The first modern factories in Myanmar, set up during the reign of the last two kings in the 19th century, were glass and steel factories, and a mint.

During the British colonial period, many industries such as rice milling and petroleum refining flourished, but these were destroyed during World War II. After the war and after independence in 1948, industries were again established by many private entrepreneurs and by the government. Private entrepreneurs were active in the textile, food and beverage, and chemical industries, while the government was involved in pharmaceuticals, cotton, jute, and steel milling. During the 1960s, private industries were nationalized by the government. Only very small private factories were left alone. In 1977, the Private Industries Law was passed; under this law, some industries, including food and beverages and clothing, were opened to private entrepreneurs.

The industrial policy of the socialist government was one of self-reliance, and efforts were made to establish industries that could substitute for foreign imports. Large industrial complexes were built such as those on the western bank of the Ayeyarwady opposite Pyi, about 180 miles (290 km) north of Yangon; the complex in Thanlyin, south of Yangon; and Daik-U, north of Yangon. Cooperatives also participated in industrial production. Because of lack of expertise and poor management and organization, these cooperatives were not terribly successful.

A state-owned garment factory. Garment-making is one industry that is open to private entrepreneurs.

35

THE MARKET ECONOMY

Despite efforts to industrialize, Myanmar's economy remains dependent on agriculture.

Since 1988 the SLORC regime has taken steps to reform the economy from a socialist economy to a market type economy. There have been efforts to open up the economy to encourage foreign investors and to increase the flow of foreign exchange into the country. However the government has been reluctant to create open policies. The economy remains mostly under government control despite claims of opening the economy. Many foreign investors who arrived in the country in the early 1990s have pulled out over the last three years. Foreign investments fell from US$161 million in 1990 to about US$70 million in 1998. The largest investors are Singapore, the UK, and Thailand. The oil and gas sector, the manufacturing sector, and the hotel and tourism sector draw the most foreign investments.

Ships on the Ayeyarwady. Myanmar factories manufacture goods mainly for local consumption—Myanmar's major export items are primary products including rice and teak.

The political standoff with Aung San Suu Kyi and her NLD party has also been a reason for investors to stay away; Aung San Suu Kyi herself asked investors to stay away from Myanmar, stating that their investments were likely to line the pockets of the ruling military. The human rights abuses alleged by international organizations such as Amnesty International have not helped to build investor confidence either.

In addition to the political climate, there remains the problem created by the overvaluation of the Myanmar currency at Ks 7 per US dollar whereas the real market value stands at Ks 400 or more per US dollar. The banking system is also outdated.

Many economic reforms are still required for the Myanmar economy to be able to achieve a high growth rate. The average growth rate of the economy over the past few years has been around 4 to 5 percent.

SOURCES OF REVENUE

Myanmar's revenue comes from the export of primary products, mainly from the export of rice and rice products. During the British colonial period, Myanmar was the largest exporter of rice in the world, exporting an average of 3.3 million tons annually. At present, however, Myanmar exports less than 0.2 million tons (1999); the economic, social, and political problems of the past two decades have caused the decline in production. Nonetheless, rice export earnings make up between 20 to 30 percent of total export earnings.

Besides rice, another major source of revenue is the export of teak and other hardwoods. Myanmar produces about 90 percent of the world's genuine teak and is believed to have at least three-quarters of the total world reserves.

Rubber, jute, corn, beans, and pulses are also major export items, as are metals and minerals such as zinc, tin, and copper.

Myanmar is also famous for gems such as jade, rubies, sapphires, and cultivated pearls, which are sold every year at the Gems Emporium to foreign gem merchants.

Total export earnings in 1998 were about $1,634 million.

Harvesting cultivated pearls, a source of revenue for Myanmar.

A woman selling brightly colored slippers. Some small traders are moonlighting civil servants.

WORK ETHIC

Traditionally, Myanmar employers have looked after their employees as a father does his children, while employees are expected to be loyal, faithful, and honest. Buddhist teaching stresses the learning of a craft or skill early in life as one of the necessary ingredients for success. Others are having good friends, spending modestly, and guarding possessions already acquired.

Resoucefulness is probably the main characteristic of the Myanmar at work. Myanmar is full of examples of this: 50-year-old buses still run, as do old cars; many machines are run with locally made parts produced from lathe machines. The isolation of the country for almost 40 years has served to reinforce this trait.

Recycling was in existence in Myanmar long before the concept became popular in the West, but it is due to necessity rather than environmental concerns. Old newspapers, books, magazines, and exercise books have a ready market. Young children scrounge near garbage piles looking for scraps of plastic that can be melted down and made into new plastic bags. Old plastic buckets, basins, and baskets can similarly be melted and molded. Used oil drums can be used for storing water or rice. In households, old bottles and cans are always saved to store sugar, salt, flour, and other kitchen ingredients. Car tires become rubber slippers.

A small family-owned cheroot-making factory.

Many private entrepreneurs have learned their business from family enterprises or from working as apprentices in other companies. They apply what they have learned and make ingenious adaptations rather than actual innovations. They are resourceful in spite of the restrictions that the private sector faces.

Public servants have few incentives to work hard since promotion is by seniority or total number of years worked. They may moonlight or do some minor trading, sell food and clothing, or lend money at interest in order to stretch a low wage. Government wages were increased in April 2000, but the inflation rate is high and thus the increase in wages is insufficient to cover consumption costs. Many also turn to bribery; people who want quick attention from public departments have to put up with this practice. At the very least, a favor is expected to be returned with another favor, and many departments work on this principle.

ENVIRONMENT

MYANMAR HAS ALWAYS BEEN proud of its vast natural resources which include land and forests, oil and gas, many kinds of gemstones, and underground minerals. Forty-five percent of the vast country is forested—one of the largest in Asia. The forests include large stands of bamboo, hardwoods, and teak in the mountain ranges and mangrove forests in the Ayeyarwady delta area. Myanmar has the largest number of teak trees in Asia.

The Myanmar economy has been deteriorating over the last few years and thus efforts to protect the environment, which include conservation of forests and underground minerals, have diminished. Fewer financial resources are also set aside for the protection of the environment.

Above: **A poor, aged Myanmar woman having a simple meal. The average per capita income is estimated at about US$300 or less per year.**

Opposite: **A floating market on the Inle Lake.**

According to statistics from the World Bank, Myanmar's population has also been living below the subsistence level. Myanmar was given Least Developed Country status in 1987 by the World Bank.

Widespread poverty has led to excessive mining, harvesting, and extreme use of resources without regard for future generations' need for the same resources.

COMMERCIAL LOGGING

Deforestation has been caused by cutting down too many trees without replanting them at an equal rate. Trees take a long time to reach maturity; for example, it takes about 100–150 years for a teak tree to attain the girth that is commercially desirable. The foreign exchange that is needed to boost the economy is mainly brought in by the exports of teak and other hardwoods. These now take first place over the rice exports which had held up the economy since the British colonial years. Exports of timber brought in US$202.6 million in 1999, about 18.3 percent of total exports. Thus deforestation is not a priority and largely ignored.

In the 1970s and 80s Myanmar had one of the lowest deforestation rates in Southeast Asia. Since 1988, however, the rate has doubled. Forest depletion has grown from 29 percent in 1961 to 49 percent in 1994.

Deforestation is also caused by the slash and burn type of shifting cultivation. This type of cultivation is used in small scale agriculture. The farmers move from one place to another, each time clearing the land by felling trees and burning the scrub before they start to plant their crops.

Another reason for deforestation is the cutting down of trees for fuel, specifically for firewood. Myanmar has not had enough energy fuel for the growing population due to distribution and policy problems and poor infrastructure. As imports of fuel, production of oil, gas, and electricity were stopped due to low foreign exchange reserves in 1997, the shortage problem has worsened in recent years.

Deforestation is one of the most destructive features of environmental abuse since it causes many ill effects on the environment. One negative side effect of deforestation is land erosion. Where the deforestation takes place on banks of rivers, the riverbanks may slide down to the river bed and cause turbidity or muddy water. This in turn affects riverine life—the fishes and waterplants and other flora and fauna living in the water of the streams and creeks. Turbidity also affects the lives of the people who depend on the river water for drinking and cooking and other purposes.

Elephants used to be the main tool for transporting logs. Now, they are replaced by huge logging machines.

The rate of deforestation has been estimated by the Myanmar government to be at 2.1 percent per annum, though independent bodies have said it is higher at 6–8 percent. The rate has been accelerated by mechanical logging procedures. New roads were created by destroying more trees than when timber was extracted by using elephants and simpler equipment.

Another factor causing accelerated deforestation is the opening up of some interior areas which had previously been inaccessible due to insurgent or rebel activities. The opening up of thickly forested areas came about because of the cease-fire agreements between the insurgent groups and the government.

The accessibility of the opened areas means that there are more hunters killing the wildlife living in these areas. Deforestation also causes changes in the migratory routes of many birds.

Among the most devastated areas are the mangrove forests in the Ayeyarwady delta.

Polishing newly made chairs.

deforestation has caused the delta to change shape, with more silting, greatly affecting the delta's marine life and the livelihood of the population.

One controversial economic venture has been the gas pipeline between Thailand and Myanmar, built to transport gas from the Gulf of Mottama gas fields. Clearning the massive areas of forests to make way for building pipes has generated much protest from environmentalists. Many villages of minority ethnic tribes are said to have been destroyed due to the gas pipeline. The habitats of fauna have also been destroyed in the process. The pipeline divided the terrain into two parts and caused dislocation for the fauna and people living in the area along the pipeline.

AIR POLLUTION

Pollution is more apparent in Yangon where there are more cars and factories. Older cars have been moved to the outlying areas and provincial towns, but car exhaust fumes in downtown Yangon areas continue to be present at very high levels. Rules and regulations concerning exhaust emission are not being strictly enforced. Garbage disposal is also a problem in the inner city with small back streets ending up as rubbish dumps.

Self-sufficiency during the socialist period required investment in heavy industries which had caused much air pollution. In addition, the continued use of obsolete equipment and machineries because of lack of capital to replace them with more energy-efficient and less polluting ones means that pollution of the environment will continue.

With the physical and population expansion of the capital, Yangon, due to the large numbers of people migrating from the rural areas in search of better employment opportunities and a more modern lifestyle, Yangon can expect much more pollution if something is not done soon. On the other hand, the entry of multinational factories and businesses that pollute the environment can also be expected with the opening up of the country unless agreements can be made from the start with these businesses, both local and foreign, regarding the protection of the environment, by the use of environmentally friendly equipment, proper waste disposal, and strict legal standards of pollution.

Exhaust fumes from cars pollute the air in Yangon.

At a time when cigarette smoking is on the wane in the developed countries, the number of people who smoke in less developed countries like Myanmar is on the rise. In Myanmar, while statistics are not available, one can see a large number of the male population lighting up all the time. Myanmar women tend to smoke cheroots, which are made of tobacco and other ingredients rolled up in corn husks. Smoking in restaurants, buildings, and offices and the careless disposal of the cigarette butts add to the pollution of Myanmar.

In addition most people have a betel chewing habit. The chewers spit out the red betel juice as they go on their way, causing unsightly red stains on roads, pavements, and walls of buildings. Some observers have put forward the view that because of lack of income and therefore lack of food, more poor people resort to smoking and betel chewing to allay their hunger.

Myanmar women smoking cheroots.

LEGAL PROTECTION OF THE ENVIRONMENT

A number of environmental laws have been enacted, most of them after the 1988 demonstrations. Among the earlier acts are the Forest Act 1902, Wildlife Protection Act 1936, and Land Nationalization Act 1953; there is now the Forest Law 1990 and the Myanmar Mines Law 1994. There are other laws such as the Canal Act, Embankment Act, and Water Power Act, the Myanmar Marine Fisheries Law, Fresh Water Fishery Law, and Aquaculture Law. The laws are there to protect the environment but the government claims enforcement of the laws is difficult because of the profit-seeking motives of private enterprises.

Enforcement of the laws would require the training and employment of a large number of rangers to protect the enormous areas to be covered with some very remote and inaccessible areas being included.

Myanmar regularly attends ASEAN meetings on the environment since the country became a member in 1997.

Public education campaigns are required to raise awareness about the problems of environment that will impact future generations. There are at present few such campaigns.

Laws have been enacted in Myanmar to protect against overfishing. Today fishermen have to apply for a license with the state office to fish within a state's waters.

THE MYANMAR

THE PEOPLE OF MYANMAR include the ethnic Bamars and many different ethnic groups such as Kayin, Shan, Kachin, Kayah, Chin, Arakanese, and the Mon. Although they are generally known as Myanmar, there are distinct differences in customs and traditions among the ethnic groups.

SOCIAL HIERARCHY

Next to the Buddhist monks, the aged receive the most respect. A Myanmar family, however impoverished, does its best to care for elderly, disabled, or sick relatives, even those quite distantly related. Homes for the aged are homes for those who have no one to care for them.

Being educated is worthy of great respect, no matter whether one has gainful employment or not. Proud parents of university graduates line living room walls with photos of their offspring in their graduation caps and gowns. A foreign degree is generally regarded as superior to local degrees and diplomas.

Among the professions, doctors and teachers are accorded high esteem. Doctors who practice for monetary fees alone are abhorred; they should be accommodating enough to accept their fees in kind, with items like bags of rice or cans of cooking oil. Relatives and close friends are "looked after" free of charge by most doctors.

At the bottom of the hierarchy are those who live on the fringes of society—beggars, lepers, and cemetery dwellers. Most of these people are taken care of by government welfare and health institutions, but a few remain outside the network.

Above: **A beggar is at the bottom of the social scale.**

Opposite: **Buddhist monks receive the greatest honor from the Myanmar. Very old monks who have lived austere and virtuous lives of spiritual rigor are especially venerated. Generally, however, it is the order of monks as a body, or the *Sangha*, rather than each individual monk, that is honored.**

ETHNIC GROUPS

Myanmar has a diverse population, the result of three separate migrations from Central Asia and Tibet. The first migration brought the Mons and the Khmers. The second group of migrants was the Tibeto-Bamars, and the third, sometime during the 13th and 14th centuries, consisted of Tai-Chinese peoples.

Bamars, or ethnic Myanmar, are the largest ethnic group, comprising 68 percent of the total population. Referred to generally as Myanmar, as opposed to the other ethnic groups, they are descendants of the Bamars, Mons, and the Tai-Chinese; typically they are dark-complexioned and tall. Predominantly Buddhists, they live mostly in the river valleys and plains.

Closely related to the Myanmar are the Mons and Rakhine (Arakanese), who are also Buddhists and mainly farmers.

A Karen family. The Karen are the third largest ethnic group in Myanmar after the Bamars and the Shan.

Karens are the third largest ethnic group; Sgaw and Pwo Karens are the two main Karen groups. They live in the Ayeyarwady delta and also in hilly Karen State. They form about 7 percent of the population.

The Shans, light-skinned and tall, are related to the Thais and the people of Laos, Cambodia, and Vietnam. Primarily farmers, they live in the river valleys and lowland pockets of the Shan plateau. They form 9 percent of the total population.

The Chin people live in Chin and Rakhine (Arakan) states. About 30 percent of the Chin have converted to Buddhism and Christianity; the rest are animists; that is, they worship spirits.

Kachins live in Kachin State in the northernmost part of Myanmar. They are well-known for their fierce fighting spirit, as are the Chin people.

Kayah people were once known as Red Kayin (Karenni) and live in Kayah State, south of Shan State.

Apart from these main groups, there are many other smaller ethnic groups such as Palaung, Padaung, Lisu, Wa, Danu, Lahu, Lashi, Yaw, and others. The smaller ethnic groups tend to live in the more remote areas of Myanmar, although many have sought refuge in other countries.

PADAUNG "GIRAFFE" WOMEN

A Myanmar lady had just arrived on a visit to London. As she unpacked, her landlady stood nearby and kept looking at the articles being laid out. Finally unable to restrain herself, she asked the visitor, "Where are your neck rings?" This landlady's misconception was probably due to posters of Myanmar showing a Padaung woman with many copper rings around her neck. Actually, the Padaung tribe numbers only a few thousand individuals who are seldom seen in the lowlands since they live in and around Loikaw, the Kayah State capital in east Myanmar. The rings are put on at an early age and increased year by year to a final total of about 20 pounds (9 kg)! This custom is said to be a deliberate deformation of the women of the tribe to prevent them from being taken by other tribes. The rings depress the collarbones and ribs and make the neck look unnaturally long. In fact, the rings cannot be removed without substituting a neckbrace, as the neck is weakened and there is a danger of suffocation otherwise.

DRESS

In place of pants and skirts, Myanmar men and women both wear sarongs called *longyi* ("lone-jee"), but tie it differently; men knot it in front and women fold it to the side. The men wear a shirt, with a small stiff collar, tucked into the *longyi*. A jacket is worn over the shirt for formal occasions. Women wear over the *longyi* an *ainygi* ("AYN-jee"), a waist-length blouse with an overlapping flap in front. For weddings and important functions, they wear a net shawl over the blouse.

A Myanmar in traditional dress.

The *longyi* worn by the men is usually checked or striped, while the women wear *longyi* with more varied designs: they may be handwoven with traditional motifs or in single colors, or they may be made from imported materials in batik or floral prints. For formal occasions silk *longyi* are essential for both men and women. Lace and brocade *longyi* are also worn by the women in the towns.

Younger girls nowadays prefer to wear western-type blouses or shirts, with a *longyi* worn calf length, which is short to Myanmar eyes! Western dresses and skirts are also worn, but this is mainly in the capital city of Yangon and in Mandalay. Shorts, skimpy blouses, and miniskirts are not approved of, generally speaking: the exposure of too much skin is considered indecent. For visits to monasteries and pagodas, Myanmar women take care to wear long sleeves and thicker materials.

Men sometimes wear headgear called *gaung baung* ("gaong-BA-ong"), a close-fitting, brimless, silk hat with a loose piece at one side.

For the Myanmar, footwear consists of a pair of thonged slippers, made of ordinary leather for everyday wear and velvet for special occasions. In the period after independence from the British, men wore shoes and socks on formal occasions, but in the ensuing socialist period that emphasized nationalism, slippers were the norm.

THE VERSATILE *LONGYI*

The men's *longyi* has all too often been a subject of curiosity because it resembles a skirt. Actually, it serves many purposes: when crossing a stretch of water or climbing a tree a man can hitch it up, gather the front portion toward the back, between the legs, and tuck it in at the waist so it becomes short pants. It can be used to wipe a sweaty face; small articles can be carried in the front knot; and young children can sit on a father's *longyi* between his legs as in a hammock. Best of all, it can be loosened after a big meal or to cool one's legs on warm days! Old worn *longyi* become rugs or cool sheets for babies to sleep on. Women can bathe with modesty at the riverside or village well by drawing their *longyi* up and wrapping it around the upper part of the body. The *longyi* keeps one's legs warm and free of mosquitoes, and sitting cross-legged is easiest in a *longyi*.

Right: **Kachin women in their traditional costumes**

Above: The Shan bag is a flat woven strip of cloth folded in two with a strap attached and is carried from the shoulder (the Kachins use a similar bag). Colorful patterns are woven into the fabric, which may be of wool, cotton, silk, or artificial fibers. Schoolchildren use it for carrying books and pencil boxes to school, as do university students. It is giving way to sling bags and attaché cases, but remains a convenient means of carrying personal articles and is easy on the shoulder. Sometimes it is slung across the chest, or the strap may be put over the forehead and the bag slung on the back.

DRESS OF THE ETHNIC GROUPS While Mon and Rakhine peoples dress the same way as the majority of the Myanmar, the other ethnic peoples of Myanmar wear many different costumes in their own states. As more young people move to urban centers in search of employment, many have opted to wear the Myanmar dress of *aingyi* and *longyi*.

Karens wear a woven striped tunic over pants or *longyi*, and a scarf is tied around the head. Shan men wear loose black pants tied as a men's *longyi*, with a shirt, while the women wear a long-sleeved, tight, hip-length jacket and a *longyi*, and also a headscarf.

Kayah women wear a cape over their shoulders and a long sash. Kachin women wear thick woolen skirts, leggings, and black blouses decorated with silver disks and tassels, and the men wear black pants and shirts. Chin women wear a woven tunic and skirt with a long shawl over the shoulders. Palaung women wear blue jackets with red collars and skirts with bamboo hoops.

HAIRSTYLES

Men's hair used to be kept long and coiled into a topknot. In the colonial period, men came to sport a short hairstyle called *bo-kay* ("boh-kay,") meaning English-style hair.

As for the women, their hairstyles have varied from dynasty to dynasty. Generally, women are expected to have long hair after they reach adulthood and keep it rolled into a bun or chignon. They love to wear flowers at the side of their buns, like a garland of jasmine or a rosebud. Fragrance is appreciated more than beauty, so the *thazin* ("THE-zin"), a delicate and tiny orchid, is highly prized for its haunting fragrance. Brides will pay a large sum to wear these flowers in their hair on their wedding day. Today, young mothers, and even older women, prefer short hair, much to the dismay of their mothers!

Before the British rule influenced them to cut their hair short, Myanmar men used to keep their hair long and coiled into a topknot.

THANAKA

Thanaka ("than-ner-KAH") is a pale yellow paste applied to the face by Myanmar women and girls. It is obtained by grinding a piece of the bark of a small tree (*Murraya paniculata*) on a circular grinding stone with a few drops of water. This paste gives a cooling effect and reduces oiliness. Grandmothers love to apply from head to toe the large amount of *thanaka* prepared by granddaughters. Young girls working in the hot sun, transplanting rice seedlings by hand, apply thick layers to keep from getting too brown. Today it can also be bought in powder or lotion form.

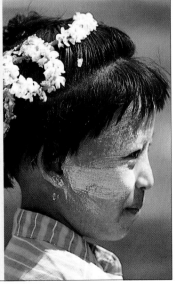

Instead of keeping their hair long and rolled into a bun or chignon as their mothers and grandmothers do, younger Myanmar women keep their hair short.

LIFESTYLE

THE MAJORITY OF MYANMAR are Buddhists and as such their attitudes and lifestyle are inevitably influenced by Buddhist beliefs.

ATTITUDES

A young child dies, the parents are grief-stricken, but they accept it as karma. A dishonest person gets cheated, a cruel person dies a gruesome death; this is the working of karma—reaping what one has sown. A Buddhist belief, deeply rooted in the Myanmar, is that everything that happens to oneself, both good and bad, is due to past deeds in this and former lives. By the same token, devout Buddhists know that any deed done in this life may affect their future rebirth. Myanmar Buddhists are afraid of *wut-ly-te* ("woot-lai-tei"), which means evil deeds follow a person without fail, in this existence and others.

Above: **Life in the village is more carefree than in the city. Here the people live off the rich land, where the forests yield wild vegetables and the creeks are full of fish.**

Opposite: **The Myanmar have a unique ability to remain cheerful even during times of great hardship.**

Myanmar are, however, cheerful, fun-loving, happy-go-lucky people who are modest and easily contented. They love a good joke and a tall tale, and are happy to spend a social evening around a pot of tea exchanging stories and anecdotes. Villagers are more carefree in that they do not worry so much about where their next meal will come from, since they have the trees and plants, and creeks full of fish on which to subsist.

In the towns, life is not as easy: there are housing problems, and essential consumer goods such as rice, soap, meat, and cooking oil are expensive and not readily available.

Myanmar hospitality is *ah-nar-hmu* at work. No unexpected visitor from out of town is turned away even when the house is full. Room is somehow made for the guest rather than causing the person the inconvenience of looking for alternative accommodations.

AH-NAR-HMU

Ah-nar-hmu ("AH-nah-hmoo"), or *ah-nar-de* is an important principle governing social relationships among the Myanmar and in their relationships with foreigners. It can roughly be defined as a feeling of hesitation in case one may be imposing a burden on another. An elderly aunt suffers in silence rather than tell her relatives that she is ill because she does not want to cause them the trouble of taking her to the doctor. A friend has borrowed some money and still has not returned it, but never will the lender ask for the borrowed money to be repaid.

Ah-nar-hmu results in white lies and beating about the bush, but most Myanmar are reluctant to cause another person trouble, loss of face, or hurt feelings. Western people with their characteristic directness are frustrated when they are unable to get a definite answer to a question, but this is mainly because a strong negative answer is always avoided by most Myanmar.

FAMILY

Family ties are strong among Myanmar. Buddhist tenets of duties and responsibilities of parents and children are still closely followed. Parents expect obedience, and children have a duty to look after parents in their old age. The act of publicly disowning a child because of an unapproved marriage is not uncommon.

In many Myanmar families you will find grandparents, uncles, aunts, and cousins living under one roof. Privacy is minimal, all disagreements and quarrels are soon known, and there are always attempts at reconciliation on the part of the elders. Everyone is expected to help in his or her own way, either by contributing toward expenses; helping with cooking, washing, and other chores; or playing the role of adviser.

Myanmar are greatly supportive of relatives, and they include those close and distant, and even close neighbors, who are referred to as "relatives from the same block." Relatives from out of town will always stay with a family rather than go to a hotel. When there are no relatives to stay with, the Myanmar visitors prefer to stay in a monastery (after requesting permission of the chief monk). In Myanmar, hotels are for foreigners.

In urban areas there are now many smaller families consisting of a couple, children, and perhaps a maid. Such parents do not receive the help and advice of their own parents as in extended families; this sometimes leads to a lower quality of family life for all concerned.

An extended Myanmar family. Life is rich in such a household, and one can always count on the support of the family in times of crises.

BIRTH

Birth is an auspicious occasion in any family. To be without children is regarded as being pitiable.

The expectant mother is required to be careful in what she eats and does; here, science and superstition appear to be well-mixed (see common taboos opposite).

In the villages, pregnant women work in the fields or in home-based industries up to the last days before giving birth. Village midwives or elderly women attend to the birth. During the last decades, government rural health centers and health assistants have been available, and traditional midwives have been gradually re-trained. In the towns, mothers receive free prenatal and postnatal care.

A child is a gift, precious to its parents.

People in rural areas have large families as each child can later contribute on the farm. There is no strong preference for boys over girls since the birth of girls does not put a heavy burden on the parents with respect to dowry at marriage. Both boys and girls are accepted as gifts of "jewel children," meaning they are precious to their parents. Girls are expected to look after their parents, while boys are likely to be "given away" to the in-laws.

It was once the tradition to bury the umbilical cord at birth and, to this day, birthplaces are referred to as "the place where the cord is buried."

The mother receives special care during the first days after delivery to clean her system, heal wounds, and make her strong again. Many callers come with gifts and good wishes to see the new baby.

The child's name is chosen within a year. A ceremony may be held when the child's hair is washed with a herbal shampoo, guests are invited, and all those who attend wish the child good health, wealth, and freedom from harm.

COMMON PREGNANCY AND BIRTH TABOOS

The pregnant mother should not eat:
 bananas or the baby will be too big for normal delivery;
 chili or the baby will have no hair;
 glutinous rice as this will make the placenta stick to the womb.
She should not attend weddings or funerals.
She should leave some things incomplete during preparation such as partially sewing baby clothes and leaving out the hems on the diapers.
After birth she should not wash her hair for about a month.
She should not eat bamboo shoots or mushrooms for some time.
She should not handle soap.

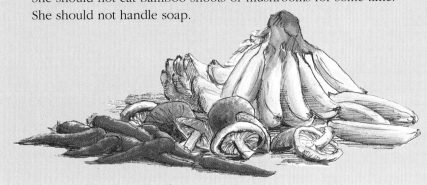

According to folklore, when a baby smiles, it is because, although jealous spirits taunt it by saying "Your mother is dead," the baby knows this is untrue since it feeds at its mother's breast daily. When a baby cries, it is because jealous spirits say, "Your father is dead," and the baby, not yet knowing the father, believes them.

CHILDREN

Most Myanmar children have a carefree childhood. Parents are indulgent toward children, giving them what they ask for if or when they can afford it. Parents and grandparents may spoil them and excuse them for mischief, saying, "They are only children!" Parents often continue to look at their children as children and not as adults even after they are married and have children of their own.

Children are taken to most places and events except for funerals. They are given a lot of attention, admired, and never ignored. They are seen and heard. Parents seldom ask the children to go away while an adults-only dinner or conversation takes place. In any case, the children soon get bored and will run away to play by themselves. In villages one can see young boys and girls smoking cheroots, and no grown-up will say anything.

Obedience is about the only thing that is expected of children. Buddhist teachings stress that when children grow up, they are obliged to look after their parents. When their parents die, children must make merits for their parents by donating money or gifts to monasteries.

In the villages or countryside, children climb trees, fish in the creeks, or go hunting in the forest. In farming

A mother and her son on their way to the fields.

communities, the boys may help by tending the cows grazing in the pasture and collecting firewood; the girls help their mothers in the house with domestic chores or looking after younger siblings. Children may go to the village monastery to learn basic Myanmar reading and writing or go to a government school. Often, children living in the rural areas have to walk several miles for this purpose.

In the towns, children may be seen playing in the streets. They may fly kites, though this is dangerous in city streets. Sometimes they run light errands for parents who run a business, or buy sweets from street vendors.

Most children in the towns go to school; some children may be needed by their parents in the family business and have to stop their schooling after primary education (at about 10 or 11 years of age). Many children earn extra pocket money by selling cigarettes, tidbits, and other goods in the streets after school hours.

Chinlon is a favorite street game for town children.

PUBERTY

At about 12 or 13 years of age, the girls are gradually segregated from the boys; no more running around, climbing trees, or following the boys. They start to wear *longyi* and *aingyi;* no more bare legs are allowed. This may be one reason why Myanmar has so few sportswomen. Girls are also expected to keep their hair longer, although this custom is slowly dying out.

Girls are expected to behave more quietly when speaking, laughing, and walking; that is, to behave with more decorum. Bathing at village wells or by the river is in the company of other girls. They are expected to help their mothers around the house, and in rural Myanmar, their formal education generally stops at this age.

At puberty or sometimes earlier, young boys go through an initiation ceremony when they wear the yellow robes of a Buddhist novice for a short period at a monastery. This ceremony is held either for a single boy or a group of them, economy and convenience being taken into consideration. During the ceremony, their heads are shaved. Then they will put on monk's robes and stay at the monastery for a few days.

During the initiation ceremony for Buddhist novices, the boys are dressed up and taken around the village or town on decorated ponies or open cars. They go to the monastery where guests and relatives are assembled. Monks are offered alms and guests are fed later. In a ceremony that follows, the boys are accepted into monkhood by the presiding monk. Their heads are shaved, and they put on monk's robes. They are required to stay a few days at the monastery, fasting and abstaining from entertainment. They are taught the scriptures, and sometimes basic meditation is practiced.

Some young girls go through a ear-piercing ceremony at the same time as their brothers and boy cousins become novices, but this ceremony does not have the same religious significance as the initiation. At this ceremony, a girl will put on court dress and have her ears pierced and earrings put on. Because of the great expense of feeding guests, this ceremony is seen much less frequently today.

Boys and girls brought up in the towns continue their education until grade 10 when there is a country-wide matriculation examination. They are about 16 to 18 years old at this time. If they pass this examination, they are able to pursue a university degree, and what they study depends on how well they did in the examination. Only those with very good results can go to medical and engineering schools.

In the 1990s, the frequent closing of schools, colleges, and universities because of student unrest interrupted the education of many young people. Hence, many students are graduating at a later age than before.

ROLE OF WOMEN

Women in Myanmar have always played an active role in the economy, whether in business, running a small roadside stall or a cheroot factory, or working the land.

Women are regarded as inferior to men in the sense that they can never be ordained as monks or become Buddhas unless they are reborn as men. Women are not allowed to enter certain parts of religious buildings such as the middle platform at the Shwe Dagon. Socially, however, their status is equal to men; if they defer to men it is due to their own wish to give men the privilege of feeling superior.

Myanmar men are believed to have *hpon* ("POH-n"), or "glory," which is thought to be diminished if they touch women's skirts and underwear and other "unclean" articles. A man cannot prosper if his *hpon* is diminished. Some families wash men's clothing separately from the women's and also iron them with separate irons. Many women do their best to adhere to this practice.

In the family it is mostly the women who take charge of the household finances. Usually the husband hands over his paycheck to be used appropriately. Women also supplement the family income in many ways, such as running a small shop in front of the house, buying and selling various articles, setting up a small business making fruit preserves or cheroots, or acting as lenders of money or brokers for the sale of jewelry.

Certain professions are regarded by parents as suitable and proper for their daughters—professions such as teaching, accounting, and secretarial work. As doctors, most become pediatricians or gynecologists because of the cultural segregation of the sexes and the taboo on touching between the sexes. Many women have broken into the ranks

of lawyers and politicians that were for a long time the preserve of men.

Nursing was once the profession entered by Christian girls who are born to a religious code of kindness towards others and selflessness. In recent years many Myanmar women have entered this profession since it brings a good income and is meaningful. At a time when many with university degrees are unemployed, young girls in their late teens and early 20s are enrolling in nursing school instead of going to a university. Most parents, however, want a university education for their daughters, and a large proportion of university students are female.

After marriage a woman keeps her own name. She may live with her parents or her in-laws. Deference is expected toward in-laws and parents, but it is not necessary for her to be around them at all times.

While divorce is not very common in Myanmar, the estimated divorce rate is said to be higher than in the 1940s. When a couple is having difficulties in their marriage, the older members of the respective families try to help the couple work things out. If there is a divorce, the woman receives half of all property acquired after marriage and whatever she originally brought to the marriage. She can also freely remarry, whether she is divorced or widowed.

Socially, women enjoy equal status with men: a large proportion of university graduates are women, and women in professional and blue-collar jobs earn the same wages as men in the same grade of appointment.

MARRIAGE

Beginning in their teens, young girls and boys are generally segregated, but they have many opportunities to meet at village activities, in school, at the university, and at work as they grow into their twenties.

Courtship customs among the Myanmar used to consist of writing love letters, initiated by the boy. In modern times the telephone has also been a means of communicating feelings. Dating usually takes place only when

A courting couple.

a girl has accepted a boy as a possible candidate for marriage. Groups of boys and girls may go out to tea shops or the movies.

Arranged marriages are still found among Myanmars. Parents hope for a person with approximately the same ethnic background, economic status, and education for their child. A go-between, who may be a relative of either party, helps.

Marriages based on mutual love are also common, but parental approval is desired and sought. Where parents cannot agree to the marriage, relatives try to help in achieving a reconciliation.

Before World War II and after independence, eligible males were mainly those in the civil service, doctors, and engineers. This is still the case, but their ranks are now increased by merchant seamen who have gained social status due to their earning power in a deteriorating economic situation.

Engagements are not really necessary, but announcements can be made in the newspapers. A small ceremony may be held at the home of the bride-to-be with parents and relatives of both parties present. The qualifications and virtues of the bride- and groom-to-be are extolled by an elder who know them well. Rings may be exchanged.

Marriage in Myanmar involves only the mutual consent of the two parties concerned. Living and eating together is enough to constitute marriage. Traditionally, the marriage is valid if neighbors recognize it as such.

Weddings can be as simple or as elaborate as the parents and the couple wish. The simplest wedding is one held before a gathering of elders in the bride's home, the bride and groom sitting together on a smooth mat paying obeisance to the Triple Gems (see page 75) and their parents. Monks may be invited and offered alms. Other couples go to the court and sign a marriage contract before witnesses and a lawyer or judge.

The most elaborate weddings are held in Yangon's hotels, where several hundred guests are invited. They are entertained by a music troupe and well-known singers before the bride and groom are married in their presence. The marriage ceremony is performed by a master of ceremonies dressed like a Brahmin. The hands of the bride and groom are tied with a silk scarf and dipped in a silver bowl of water. Conch shells are blown and silver coins and confetti are scattered over the guests. Refreshments are served after the ceremony, usually tea with cakes, sandwiches, and ice cream. The bride and groom then go around and talk to the guests and accept congratulations.

Modern couples go on honeymoons to resort beaches or to highland resorts such as Pyin oo lwin (Maymyo) and Taunggyi.

Newlyweds usually live with the bride's parents for a short while before moving into their own home.

DEATH

To the Myanmar, death is accepted as just one stage in the life cycle. The dead person is simply leaving his or her body behind to move on to a new rebirth in the endless cycle of existence. The family grieves, but not for a long period of time. No mourning periods are specified.

When a person dies while away from home—for example, on the way to the hospital—the body is not allowed back into the village or street quarter. It is common to see just outside the village boundary a corpse in its coffin laid out for burial.

On the day a person dies, the family invites a monk to the family's monastery and makes an offer of food to indicate that a life has been lost. The dead person is bathed and dressed in his or her favorite clothes. Candles, incense sticks, water, and token offerings of food are placed at the head. An earthen water pot is placed under the bed on which the body is laid.

The spirit of the dead is believed to be still in and near the residence up to a week after death. There is a wake that lasts a whole week. Doors and windows are kept open throughout this period. In villages, all the villagers help. The youths help by staying awake through the night and letting the family members, exhausted by grief and by talking to callers the whole day, take a rest. The young people stay awake by playing cards, drinking plain tea, and eating snacks. Other neighbors assist in cooking the food for the family and other helpers.

A week later, monks are invited again to be given alms, to pray, and to remind the spirits of the deceased that they are no longer members of

The funeral of a young girl outside the village. The coffin is decorated this way to ward off ghosts and spirits.

the household and must go their own way. All merits (good deeds that lead to a better life now or in future existences) are shared with them in order that they might be reborn to a better life.

At the funeral, the height of each member of the family is measured with thread; the lengths of thread are then put into the coffin. A 25-*pya* ("PIAH") coin is placed in the mouth of the deceased to be used as payment to the ferryman when crossing to the land of the dead. The water pot is broken. The grief of the bereaved reaches a climax, and there is no restraint in weeping and lamenting; it is believed that the relief of crying is healthy for the bereaved. Burial is usual in Myanmar, but in Yangon cremation is common. The ashes of the dead are usually not collected after cremation as they are among other cultures.

The *pyattaik*, or celestial chariot, bears the body of a monk, on the third day of the funeral, to the top of a high hill from which he ascends to heaven from a pyre of fragrant sandalwood, accompanied by fireworks.

Among the ethnic groups, the Buddhist Karens living in the Kayin State perform a bone collection ceremony a year after death. The bones of the dead are collected and placed in a special hut, and food and prayers are offered.

In the villages, very simple markers are used for graves, and there is generally no effort to maintain graves or a day such as All Souls' Day. Instead, the dead are remembered at feasts offered to monks for the purpose of sharing merit with them. Many other good deeds, such as donations to homes for the aged, donating scripture books, building monasteries, and food offerings, may be done by the remaining members of the family to help the dead on their way along the cycle of existence.

RELIGION

THE PREDOMINANT FAITH in Myanmar is Buddhism, but other faiths exist.

BUDDHISM

Eighty-five percent of Myanmar's population is Buddhist; this includes about 99 percent of the Myanmar, Shans, and Karens. The Buddhism practiced in Myanmar is Theravada Buddhism, similar to that found in Thailand, Laos, Sri Lanka, and Cambodia, and different from the Mahayana Buddhism of China, Japan, Korea, Tibet, Nepal, and Vietnam.

The Buddha was not a god but a human being, a prince of a kingdom in India who lived more than 2,500 years ago. He renounced the material world at the age of 29 to look for a cure for the ills of the world, including disease, old age, and death. He practiced various methods for a period of six years until he gained Omniscience, or Enlightenment, having understood the Four Noble Truths and found the Middle Way, or Eightfold Path, a guideline to escape from the sufferings of all people.

Above: **The Buddha preaching the Four Noble Truths in the very first sermon after his Enlightenment.**

Opposite: **Buddhism strongly influences life in Myanmar. Every day, one finds many devotees in prayer or quiet meditation at the temples and pagodas.**

THE FOUR NOBLE TRUTHS

The Four Noble Truths discerned by the Buddha on reaching Enlightenment are, first, that all life involves pain—suffering, birth, disease, old age, and death. No matter how wealthy one may be, one cannot escape any of these ills. Second, the reason for these ills is craving, desire, or attachment to things, pleasures, and people. Third, detachment can bring an end to pain and an escape from the cycle of rebirths. Fourth, detachment can be achieved by following the Eightfold Path.

BUDDHIST PHILOSOPHY The basic philosophy of Buddhism is that the Universe and all forms of life in it are in a constant process of change, from birth to death. After death, there is rebirth; the cycle of death and rebirth is endless. There are 31 planes of existence into which beings can be born depending on their karma, which is the result of their thoughts, deeds, and speech. Some of these planes of existence are the animal plane, the ghost planes, the human plane, and the celestial planes.

The law of karma is a law of cause and effect: whatever happens to one is the result of one's past actions—including thought, deeds, and speech—in previous existences, and one can expect to reap the result of one's actions in this existence, in this life or future lives. The ideal goal of a Buddhist should be to reach Nirvana ("nir-VAH-nah") and make a complete severance from the cycle of existences. Nirvana is defined as an extinction of greed, anger, and delusion (belief in ego or self). The way to reach Nirvana is to acquire morality, concentration, and wisdom, or insight, by following the Eightfold Path.

The *Tripitaka*, or Three Baskets, is the Buddhist scripture.

THE EIGHTFOLD PATH

The Eightfold Path consists of right understanding, right thought, right speech, right action, right livelihood, right effort, right mindfulness, and right concentration. There are strict definitions of what constitutes "right"; right speech, for example, means refraining from empty chatter, gossip, and abuse.

BUDDHIST WORSHIP The Buddhists worship the Triple Gems that are the Buddha, the *Dhamma*, or his teaching, and the *Sangha*, or his disciples, the monks. The *Dhamma*, which means truth or law, consists of the scriptures known as the *Tripitaka* (Three Baskets). Buddhists cannot beseech the Buddha for fulfillment of wishes. They do all they can to gain merit by keeping the five precepts of abstaining from killing any living beings, stealing, adultery, lying, and taking intoxicants; and occasionally, the eight precepts that include celibacy, avoiding entertainment and adornment, and sleeping on luxurious beds. These are only the fulfillment of morality. For wisdom and concentration, they have to practice meditation in any one of 40 methods.

OTHER FAITHS

Buddhists form the majority of the population in Myanmar, but there are Christians, Hindus, Muslims, Chinese Taoists, Confucians, Jews, and animists.

The earliest conversions to Christianity took place around the early 17th century. A significant number of Karens, Chin, Kachin, and Myanmar are Baptists. Christian missionaries were active from the colonial period up to the mid-1960s, establishing schools and running hospitals and social welfare centers, which were of high standards and provided good quality services. After 1962 these establishments were nationalized by the government.

The *Sangha* is the order of monks whose role is to spread the teaching of the Buddha, give guidance in meditation methods, and confirm the layperson's belief or confidence in the Buddha and the *Dhamma*. Monks enter the order at any age, subject to some conditions, and can remain as long as they wish. They follow a strict set of 227 rules of conduct, keep 10 precepts, which include no food after noon, no handling of money, no entertainment, and celibacy. They are forbidden to practice skills such as medicine and astrology, that may be used wrongly to gain followers or donations.

Right: **Pagodas have eight planetary posts at the eight compass points for each day of the week plus an extra day created by dividing Wednesday into two days. Each day is characterized by an animal. For the Myanmar, the day of the week on which one is born is as important as one's birth date.**

Below: **A household shrine.**

PLACES OF WORSHIP

To a visitor, every hilltop in Myanmar appears to have a pagoda on the summit, even if it is small and only whitewashed. Myanmar has often been called the Land of Pagodas. Even Mount Victoria, Myanmar's third highest peak, has a pagoda on its peak, 10,000 feet (305 m) up. Pagodas are usually built high up since they contain holy relics and therefore should never be on a level lower than people's houses.

Pagodas are solid conical structures with a central treasure vault below. A terrace around the pagoda provides pilgrims with space for praying, meditating, or making offerings. Temples are built with a hollow chamber in the center unlike pagodas, and pilgrims can enter the temple. Other Buddhist structures include Buddha images built in the open or under a shelter. A *Dhamma-yone* ("Der-mah-yohn") is a place where sermons and feasts are held.

Entrances to large pagodas and temples are lined with small stalls where people sell flowers and sprigs of leaves, candles, gold leaf, small paper umbrellas, streamers, and fans to be offered to the Buddha. It is the custom to remove shoes and slippers on entering these places, as a sign of respect. Myanmar women wear a brown shawl or scarf that is wrapped around one shoulder across to the waist when praying.

Monasteries are places where monks reside, but people may also go there to pay their respects and offer alms of food and provisions, money, and robes. They may spend a whole day or several days at a monastery observing the precepts and meditating in one of the *zayat* ("zer-YAHT"), meaning resting place, in the grounds. Many religious feasts, including those for novitiation and robe-offering ceremonies, are held in monasteries. Women are forbidden to enter some parts of a monastery.

This Anglican church in the hill station of Pyin oo lwin was built by the British.

Every Buddhist household has a shrine in the living room, either built into a wall or placed on a high table or cupboard. Images of the Buddha, some of which may have belonged to ancestors, are placed together with images of Buddha's disciples and pictures of famous pagodas, monks, and relics. Flowers, candles, votive water, and food are offered daily.

In Myanmar, faiths other than Buddhism are also freely worshiped and one can find churches, cathedrals (such as the famous Holy Trinity and St. Mary's), mosques, Hindu temples, and Chinese temples in Yangon and many other towns in the country.

HOLY SYMBOLS AND RELIGIOUS RITES

Myanmar Buddhists show reverence to the Buddha by keeping the Buddha's image in their household shrine and offering flowers, candles, water, and food. The food is a token portion from a newly cooked pot of rice, a new cake, or fruit just bought and washed. The food is offered at dawn or in the early morning and thrown away at noon. Flowers are changed as they wither, and water is changed daily. The Buddha's image is a visual aid that reminds the Buddhist that the Buddha really lived over 2,500 years ago and was a Supreme human being. It confirms a person's confidence or belief in the teaching of the Buddha.

Buddhists hold their palms together in reverence when they pass a pagoda or meet monks. Pagodas are sacred because most of them contain relics of the Buddha inside their central vault. Books and pictures of Buddha are also sacred; these should never be placed underfoot or stepped over. Buddha images should never be lower than head level. It upsets Buddhists to see images of the Buddha placed at the foot of stairs as decoration, inside bookshelves, and even used as umbrella stands.

Banyan trees are seldom cut down; instead, small *nat* (spirit) shrines are built on or near them.

The banyan tree is holy because it is the tree under which the Buddha reached Enlightenment; banyan trees are seldom cut down. Small shrines are built on their trunks, and flowers and candles are offered. Drooping branches of the banyan are sometimes propped up with bamboo poles to earn merit for a sick or dying person.

When misfortune comes to a family, it is common to invite monks to the home, offer them alms, and request them to recite the *paritta,* or scriptures, which are believed to have the power to overcome dangers, disease, and misfortune. Flowers, water in a bowl, sand, and spools of thread are placed before the monks. After the recitation, the water may be drunk as holy water, the sand sprinkled around the outside of house, and the thread cut up whenever necessary and tied around objects in the house or around the wrists of children to ward off evil.

After prayers, a devotee beats a small triangular gong with a small wooden mallet or rings a bell as a symbol of sharing merit with all beings.

A 24-petaled chrysanthemum is the symbol of the *Paticcasamuppada,* the Law of Dependent Origination, one of the topics preached by the Buddha, and sometimes to symbolizes *Pathana,* the 24 Causal Relations. Golden umbrellas are placed on hearses of those who have built pagodas and monasteries during their lifetime.

Above: **A 24-petaled chrysanthemum is used as a symbol of the Law of Dependent Origination, the cyclic chain in which beings are reborn again and again, and from which they are unable to escape.**

Left: **After prayers, a devotee strikes a small triangular gong as a symbol of sharing merit with all beings.**

FOLK BELIEFS

In spite of centuries of Buddhist practice, animism, the worship of spirits that has existed from an even more remote time, continues to exist alongside Buddhism. Ghosts and demons have not been seen by many, but that is no reason to disbelieve those who claim to have seen them.

At a festival, an offering of bananas, rolled tobacco leaves, and other foods is made to the *nat*.

The Myanmar spirit world has 37 *nats*, or spirits. Most of these are spirits of those who have died a violent death. Shrines are built for them and offerings made. Most of these spirits are appeased out of fear, for they are capable of punishing more than rewarding. That does not mean, however, that one cannot ask for health, fame, or fortune.

Even among those who have given up animistic worship, a spell of bad luck and a visit to an astrologer can make them revert back to their traditional *yoe-yar* worship to appease spirits that still want their offerings.

For *nat* worship, it is the custom to hang a green coconut in a small basket in a corner of the living room. If there is an illness, for example, and the stem of the coconut is found to be dry, it is assumed that the spirit is angry because the coconut has not been replaced by a fresh one. Those who work on the stage, make movies, or play in orchestras customarily need to offer bananas, coconut, and tobacco leaves to the spirit of the arts before performances.

Cursing for a person to die, even in jest, is frowned on; statements such as, "Bye-bye, I'm going and not coming back again," and similar words are believed to be omens of death and bad luck. Children are admired, but one should never say how fat, tall, or healthy they are in case the spirits get jealous and make them sick. Nor should one say, "I never get sick, never catch a cold." Wives should not wash their hair when their husbands are away. Hair should not be washed or cut on Monday, Friday, or the day of one's birth. Hair should not be washed in the evenings or let down loose after dark. Pots should not be banged with ladles, as this may invite hungry ghosts. Clothes should not be put on back to front during play (corpses are dressed this way). Children should not hide inside rolls of mats.

Woodcutters and hunters who live off the jungle are very careful with their language so as not to anger forest spirits. Fishermen and miners have their own spirits to worship. Some places are believed to have particularly powerful spirits, and visitors are warned not to anger them by making jokes or belittling them as they can make one lose one's way and cause other trouble. One should never say, "come along, everyone," when passing cemeteries, as ghosts may follow.

As the belief in rebirth is widespread, Myanmar children born with peculiar traits will draw comments regarding to their previous existence. Similarly, an animal that exhibits human-like characteristics is said to be "close to human existence." There are many stories of people who are reborn in neighboring villages (they have mannerisms or traits of those who have died), and those who are able to recall their previous lives.

Myanmar tradition states that one should not have a haircut on Monday, Friday, or one's birthday.

MAGIC

Black magic or sorcery is widely believed in, especially in villages. Villagers may be afraid of someone who seems to possess magical powers. Spells may be cast on children and adults, sometimes not out of malice or anger but out of love. Bad spells can be cured by those who have the power to undo the spell and punish the perpetrator. These people are not monks but lead virtuous lives in order to possess the power to drive away evil spirits. They give charms such as holy thread and holy water, or make offerings to prevent or break a spell. A spell may manifest itself in illness or strange behavior that cannot be cured by conventional medicine. If a person dies and a spell is suspected, it is usual to cremate the body; the spell is said to remain unburnt in the ashes.

Spells may be hidden in food, which is then fed to unsuspecting victims, or they may be buried in the victim's garden or under the house. These spells, called "*inn*," are pieces of slate, wood, bone, or foil on which squares are made and filled in with letters or numbers. The very same kind of "inn," but "good" ones, are dispensed by astrologers to deflect any bad luck. The squares are placed on altars, and lit candles are placed on them.

Besides "magicians," clairvoyants, astrologers, and palmists abound in Myanmar. They are consulted by those who wish for certainty at some point in their lives. When a clairvoyant's powers become known, people line up at the doorstep to learn about their own future.

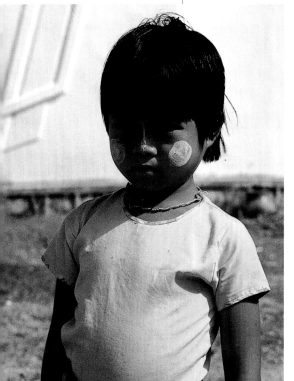

Very young children wear holy thread around their necks or wrists to protect them from bad spirits or spells.

Astrologers are consulted to pick auspicious days for weddings or ground-breaking ceremonies or identify days on which to be cautious. To change the luck of a person, an astrologer may offer a change of name or advise offering certain flowers and leaves to the Buddha. He may advise on the kind of merit one should make; for example, the number of birds and fishes to set free, the number of rounds of rosary to say, or the kinds of food to avoid.

Astrologers and palmists may be found on the streets and on pagoda grounds. Large posters and big banners announce their names and advertise their claims of being able to predict winning numbers in the state lottery, a marriage partner, and even future existences.

A sidewalk palm reader in Yangon. Palmists and astrologers are consulted by those who wish for certainty at some point in their lives.

LANGUAGE

THE MYANMAR LANGUAGE BURMESE belongs to the Tibeto-Bamar language group. To a foreign ear Burmese sounds much like Chinese. It is monosyllabic and tonal; mispronunciation of tones results in meaningless sentences. Burmese is the official language in Myanmar.

SPOKEN LANGUAGE

Spoken Burmese differs from region to region; some regional accents are quite strong. In regions such as the eastern state of Rakhine (Arakan), and Dawei and Myeik in the south, the dialects spoken are forms of old Burmese.

The young people in Myanmar speak slang, which is frowned upon by the older people as being coarse and decadent. However, slang continues to be a popular medium of communication among the younger generation, and its usage is reinforced by comic books, cartoons, novels, and popular songs.

As Myanmar was once a British colony, most Myanmar can speak, or at least understand, simple English. Those Myanmar who were of school age during the Japanese occupation are able to speak simple Japanese.

The ethnic groups speak their own languages. The Kachin, Chin, and Kayin have Romanized alphabets developed by the early missionaries. The Shan and Mon also have their own writing. Most Myanmar are unable to speak the ethnic languages, while ethnic groups have learned to speak Burmese.

Above: Ethnic groups, including the Akhas, speak their own languages, although they have learned to speak Burmese well.

Opposite: Burmese script on a street sign.

FORMS OF ADDRESS

For the Myanmar, how one addresses or speaks to a person depends on his or her age and social status. When addressing monks, one must use a special form of speech. Elders, teachers, doctors, and those worthy of respect are addressed in polite form. Honorific titles must be used with such persons, while among equals—in age or social status—a freer form of speech is used. "Ko" and "Daw" are used for addressing adult men and women, respectively; "Maung" is used for younger men, and "Ma" for young women. "Saya" is used for teachers, doctors, or one's employer; "sayama" being the feminine form.

FIRST ENGLISH-BURMESE DICTIONARY

The first English-Burmese dictionary was compiled during the middle of the 19th century by Adoniram Judson (1788–1850), an American Baptist missionary. Judson had arrived in Myanmar in 1813. In 1824, during the second Anglo-Myanmar war, he was imprisoned with other foreigners in the capital of Innwa and was released a year later.

Judson completed the English-Burmese dictionary in 1849; a Burmese-English dictionary remained unfinished at the time of his death. It was completed only in 1852 by another missionary, E.O. Stevens. These two dictionaries are still in use today.

OLD BURMESE MANUSCRIPTS

In the past, the Myanmar wrote on paper, lacquered boards, and palm leaves. A Burmese book of prayer, or *parabaik,* may be eight feet (2.4 m) long and 18 inches (46cm) wide and folded like a concertina, each fold being about six inches (15cm) long and eight inches (20 cm) wide. Palm-leaf manuscripts, or *pay-sar*, are palm leaves that are trimmed, sewn, and folded, and written on with a metal stylus. Religious, literary, and scientific works, letters, and horoscopes were in the form of palm leaf manuscripts. Lacquer manuscripts, or *kammavaca*, contain Buddhist scriptures in Pali, written in a square script.

BURMESE SCRIPT

The Burmese alphabet consists of 33 letters that are combined with various symbols to indicate the tones. The letters are circular in appearance. These letters were originally square, derived from rock-cut scripts of south India, but have gradually become rounded.

While the alphabet was derived from the Pallva script of South India, it did not come directly from the original source. The Myanmar obtained their alphabet from the Mons of ancient Thaton, who had earlier received religious teachings in Pali, possibly from the fifth century Buddhist center in Kanchipuram (Madras).

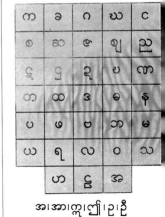

The Burmese alphabet and vowels.

MYANMAR NAMES

To those used to a system of family names, Myanmar names are very confusing because surnames are entirely unnecessary. At the workplace there may be a number of persons having the same name, in which case it is perhaps more expedient to give them numbers! In one organization in Rangoon, there are about 20 U Maung Maungs. Most parents go by the Myanmar name-choosing method where each day of the week is assigned the various letters of the alphabet; parents choose a name beginning with any of the letters belonging to the day on which the child is born.

CHOOSING A NAME THE MYANMAR WAY

Letters assigned to the different days of the week are:

Monday	– ka, kha, ga, nga
Tuesday	– sa, hsa, za, nya
Wednesday	– wa, la
Thursday	– pa, hpa, ba, ma
Friday	– tha, ha
Saturday	– ta, hta, da, na
Sunday	– a

U Ba Khin (Thursday-born) and wife Daw Khin Khin (Monday-born) might name their Friday-born daughter Ma Thet Thet. Care has to be taken in picking the name since certain combinations of letters are supposed to be favorable and others bring bad luck to a person.

ASTROLOGY AND NAMES

Some parents name their child with the help of an astrologer. This person makes astrological calculations and chooses a name designed to lessen bad aspects foreseen and bring good fortune to the child.

It is also quite common for people to change their names in mid-life on the advice of an astrologer in order to change their luck for the better. In such circumstances, the way to establish an identity is to ask who the parents are, where they come from or live, what work they do, and so on, until one can place a person.

အမည်ပြည့်စွက်ခြင်း

ဦးကြီးမြင့် (ခ) ဦးသူတော်၏ သား ဦးအောင်ဒင်အဖျိုးသားမှတ်ပုံတင် အမှတ် **LLM-006379** ဆား ယနေ့မှ စ၍ ဦးအောင်ဒင်(ခ)ဦးခင်စိုးဟုပြည့်စွက်ခေါ် ကြပါရန်။

An advertisement in the newspaper announcing a change of name. "U Aung Din, national registration no. LLM 006379, son of U Thu Daw, will from today henceforth be known as U Aung Din (aka) U Khin Soe."

NICKNAMES

Nicknames are quite common, especially in childhood. These nicknames are given in the spirit of love and humor; a very dark child might be called Maung Mai, or Master Blackie. Some nicknames are deliberately demeaning—a very sickly child may be called Maung Than Chaung, or Master Iron Bar, just so that he might grow stronger and sturdier.

In many families the children are nicknamed by their position in the family: Ko Ko (big brother), Ma Ma (big sister), Nyi Nyi (younger brother), and Nyi Ma Lay (youngest sister).

NONVERBAL LANGUAGE

The Myanmar are an informal people, but they do consider it important that due respect be shown to elders and those of higher social status, not only in speech but also in posture. For example, when older people are on a mat it is not decent for a younger person to be sitting on a chair. Similarly, to pass objects over the heads of elders is disrespectful; when handing an object to an elderly person, the left hand is held at the right elbow to show respect. To talk to an elder who is sitting at a lower level, the younger party will slightly bow from the standing position. When passing in front of elders, respect is shown by walking past, bowing slightly. In passing pagodas, or meeting monks, one holds one's palms together as a gesture of reverence.

The *kadawt* gesture is a way of honoring one's elders.

The Myanmar show their respect for parents, grandparents, teachers, and those to whom gratitude is due with the *kadawt* ("ker-dorht") gesture, a way of honoring and also asking for forgiveness of any thoughtless acts. Kneeling, with palms held together, one crouches down to the floor, touching it with forehead and elbows. This gesture, like a small ceremony, is made when younger people are going on a journey or when some older person is leaving, on some festival day when a favor has been received from a superior, and when an old person dies.

The head and hair of a person are held reverent, and the feet are the lowliest part of the body. A Myanmar in his office will never put his feet

MYANMAR SMILE

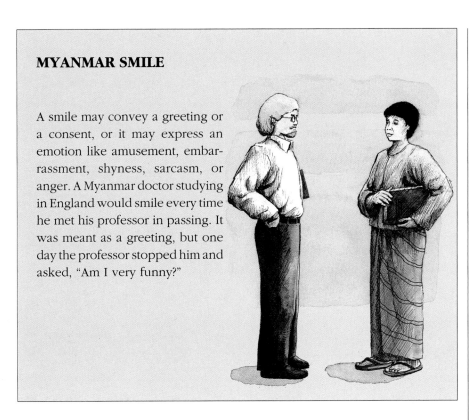

A smile may convey a greeting or a consent, or it may express an emotion like amusement, embarrassment, shyness, sarcasm, or anger. A Myanmar doctor studying in England would smile every time he met his professor in passing. It was meant as a greeting, but one day the professor stopped him and asked, "Am I very funny?"

on his desk, and to use the feet in pointing or kicking is very rude. Shoes and slippers have to be removed when entering Myanmar homes, monasteries, or pagodas.

Although women are accorded equal status with men, they are not allowed to enter certain places such as the higher levels of pagodas. Their garments, especially their *longyi*, are never hung out in front of the house or overhead.

Most Myanmar are embarrassed by any show of affection in public. Touching is generally taboo between the sexes, even among members of a family. On the beach, one will not see any young Myanmar man with a woman taking a ride on his shoulders. At religious congregations, women are seated separately from the men.

ARTS

LIKE SO MANY aspects of Myanmar life, the arts are closely tied to the Buddhist way of life and teachings.

TRADITIONAL DRAMA

Many Myanmar people love to watch a classical drama known as *zat* ("ZAHT"). This is based on the 550 *Jataka* tales told by the Buddha in which he describes his past existences and encounters with relatives, disciples, and enemies. In these tales, the Buddha's heroic deeds, wisdom, and courage—before he had achieved Enlightenment—are portrayed. The *zat* takes all night to perform and is punctuated by dancing and singing. The dancers themselves sing, or a backstage vocalist is used.

The *zat* is performed in a *zat-yone*, a large bamboo structure with a stage, or in an open-air area with a bamboo matting fence. The *zat* starts about midnight and finishes at sunrise. In the earlier part of the evening, there are short dances.

The audience sits on mats, which have to be bought at a few kyats per mat. A family needs four to six mats if children, grandparents, and others are included. They bring food, usually snacks such as *lepet* (pickled tea)—which helps to keep them awake—beverages, cheroots, and *betel* for chewing. Young babies are taken along and breast-fed while their mothers watch the play. It is common to see people dozing off now and then.

Another well-known drama is the *yamazat*, a Myanmar version of the Hindu epic *Ramayana*. It is performed by actors wearing masks. The principal characters are Princes Yama and Lekkhana, the brothers; Princess Thida, the ogre, and Hanuman, the monkey.

Above: **A village holds an all-night-long *zat* on the occasion of a pagoda festival. Before the play begins, the audience is entertained by short dances.**

Opposite: **The *Jataka* tales, told by Buddha about his existence before Enlightenment, are depicted here on a wall mural in the Lokahteikpan temple in Bagan.**

THE MARIONETTE THEATER

The marionette theater probably originated in the late 18th century during the time of King Nga Sint Gu Min, although there is some evidence that it existed during the Innwa period (mid-17th century). The minister for royal entertainment, U Thaw, is considered its originator. Social relationships between the sexes were so restricted at that time that puppets substituting for real actors became popular and the marionette theater flourished.

The Myanmar marionette theater has all but disappeared with the emergence of other performing arts. Today it can only be seen at some pagoda festivals.

Myanmar marionettes require great skill to manipulate, since some of them may have as many as 60 strings. Some puppets can even move their eyebrows! The marionette show must have 28 characters: a king, an old woman, a prince, a princess, two princes regent (one white-faced and the other red), one astrologer, one hermit, one *nat* (spirit), one *mahadeva* ("mer-HAH-day-va," meaning deity), one old man, two buffoons, two worshipers, a horse, two elephants (one black and one white), a tiger, a monkey, two parrots, one dragon, a wizard, and four ministers. The puppet masters manipulate their puppets, while female and male impersonators sing and recite the parts.

The marionette theater has almost vanished as the emergence of other performance arts has drawn audiences away and the demand for this type of theater has decreased. When performers and old puppet masters die, there are no new masters to take their places. At present, the marionette show is very rare and can be seen only at some pagoda festivals.

MODERN THEATER

The *pya-zat* (*pya* means "to show" and *zat* means "story") is a relatively modern, musical stage play with many songs and a simple plot.

Unlike a Western musical, however, there is usually no dancing. Speech is in simple prose, whereas in traditional drama parts are spoken in verse and recited. The *pya-zat* started as a mime known as "live bio-scope," because it imitated the silent movies but involved live actors. It was popular before World War II and after independence, with the increasing popularity of motion pictures in the 1950s, *pya-zat* slowly disappeared.

The late appearance of this type of play, in the 1930s, has been attributed to the social taboos during the conservative Konbaung period, which, among other things, forbade a man and woman to be seen together in public unless they were husband and wife.

In 1943, a number of theater halls were built in Yangon. The plays were performed on stage, and orchestras played below the stage. Between 1943 and 1969, over 200 plays were staged, of which about 180 were musical plays. These *pya-zat* are now being revived by the present government and play to full houses.

Theaters showing movies from the West are popular, especially among the younger generation in Yangon. During weekends, many young people can be seen hanging around the theaters.

Billboard advertising of the latest movies. The increase in popularity of the movie theater in the 1950s led to the decline of other theaters such as marionette theater and the *pya-zat.*

DANCE

Myanmar dance has existed from pre-Buddhist times when *nat* (spirit) worship was performed with dance. Dance movements were strongly influenced by classical Indian and Thai dance. Myanmar dance is rather vigorous and requires some difficult acrobatic feats. It is also quite decorous; male and female dancers do not touch when dancing together. Young beginners are taught the *ka-bya-lut* ("ker-biah-LOOT"), a basic traditional dance.

An interesting dance is one in which dancers perform like puppets. It has been said that Myanmar dance had to be copied from puppets because the marionette theater had replaced human dancers for a period. The principal female dancer wears a court dress with a bodice and long-sleeved jacket that has stiff curved edges at the hips; the *longyi* has a train that the dancer kicks out as she dances. Principal male dancers dress as princes in silk *longyi*, jacket, and white headdress. Other roles include pages, soldiers, *zawgyi* ("zor-jee," meaning wizard), and *nat*.

The *yein* is a popular dance at the Water Festival celebrations. It involves uniformly dressed dancers, usually female, dancing in unison, The *hna-par-thwa* ("ner-PAH-THWAH") is a duet dance between a male and female. The elephant dance, performed at the Elephant Dance Festival in Kyaukse near Mandalay, has the dancers in a papier-mâché and bamboo-frame elephant costume.

The *anyein* ("er-NYAYN") is a combination of solo dancing and clowning by *lu-pyet* ("loo-pi-yairt"), or clowns. The clowns sing, dance, compose impromptu speech, and make jokes about current events and various other topics, some of which are quite bawdy. During the intervals when the clowns appear, the dancer rests or changes her costume. Sometimes two or more dancers take turns dancing. The entire performance lasts about two hours.

Many of the ethnic dances are performed with swords or different kinds of drums. Ethnic dances include group dancing in which young boys and girls dance together, which is not very common in Myanmar dance.

The Elephant Dance Festival in Kyaukse near Mandalay. The dance may also be seen at big village festivals.

MUSIC

Myanmar music can be disconcerting to the Western ear with its various separate sounds from drums, gongs, cymbals, bamboo clappers, flute, and oboe. The sounds are in sharp contrast rather than in harmony.

When the Myanmar king Hsinbyushin Min invaded and conquered Siam (Thailand) in the 18th century, many Siamese musicians, dancers, composers, and craftspeople were brought to Myanmar. Myanmar culture and music has been greatly influenced by this augmentation. A type of classical song and dance is known as *yodaya,* meaning Siamese. Western musical instruments such as the violin, piano, mandolin, guitar, and accordion have also been incorporated into Myanmar music over the decades.

The Myanmar orchestra consists of a drum circle, gong circle, bamboo clappers, wind instruments including a *hne* ("h-NAIR")—which has a high-pitched sound—flute, and cymbals. Apart from the drum circle, there is also a large drum hung from an ornamental winged dragon.

The drum and gong circles are bright and colorful, decorated with glass mosaic and gold paint; they can be taken apart to be transported and reassembled at the performance location. There are 21 drums in a large drum circle, nine in a small drum circle. A gong circle has 19 gongs. Sometimes, instead of a gong circle, there is a gong rectangle that consists of a row of gongs hung in a rectangular frame; this has fewer gongs than a gong circle.

A Myanmar orchestra performing at a pagoda festival.

Different kinds of drums are used for different celebrations. The *sidaw* ("see-dor," or large drum) is for important formal occasions, the *ozi* ("OH-zee," meaning pot-shaped drum) and *dobat* ("doh-baht," meaning two-faced drum) are for village celebrations, and the *bonshay* (long drum) and *bongyi* ("bohn-JEE," meaning big drum) are for ploughing and harvesting festivals. A Myanmar drum is tuned with a piece of dough made of boiled rice and wood ash, which is stuck to the base of the drum to determine its tone. A melody can be played on the drum circle as the drums have different tones.

The *saung-gauk* ("SAONG-goak") Myanmar harp is a 13-stringed instrument shaped like a boat. The harpist sits and holds the harp in the lap when playing. Classical songs are accompanied by the harp. The *puttalar* ("PAHT-ter-LAH") xylophone is made of wooden or bamboo pieces.

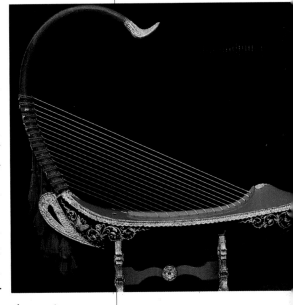

A beautifully carved Myanmar harp.

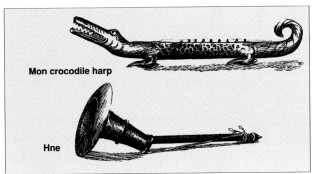

Mon crocodile harp

Hne

There are many ethnic musical instruments and they vary in shape and material. The Chin have an oboe-like instrument, the *bu-hne* ("BOO-hnair"), which is a gourd containing a number of bamboo reeds. The Mon gong circle is a curved horseshoe shape lined with gongs. The Kayah have a bamboo flute with different lengths of bamboo attached to each other in a triangular shape.

LITERATURE

The earliest Myanmar literature was primarily of a religious nature and was inscribed on stone. These inscriptions go as far back as the Bagan period in the 11th century.

Palm-leaf manuscripts and folded paper manuscripts came into existence only after the 15th century. The literature during this period was mainly concerned with the *Jataka* tales told by the Buddha to his disciples in answer to certain questions. It was in the form of drama and epistles or missives, written in verse. Works on law and history were written in prose. Many dramas were written during the 16th to 18th centuries, while in the 19th century, poems, drama, and chronicles were produced.

After Myanmar fell to the British, the country's literature began to reflect the impact of a Western culture; the arrival of the printing press also influenced literature, which previously had been written for a much smaller audience. Plays that had been written for the court became widely available; these plays were not performed on the stage but were meant to be read.

Novels were a later development; the first Myanmar novel was an adaptation of Alexander Dumas' *The Count of Monte Cristo*, but written in a Myanmar setting.

Myanmar classical literature is flowery with long, difficult sentences and is concerned with the supernatural and magical. Originating from the court of the Myanmar kings, it was greatly influenced by Buddhist Pali and Sanskrit sources.

MYAZEDI INSCRIPTION

The Myazedi inscription is a four-sided stone inscription executed in A.D.1113 by Prince Rajakumara. It records the merit of the building of a pagoda in Bagan by the prince for his dying father, King Kyansittha. The inscription is written in Burmese, Pyu, Mon, and Pali and was discovered in 1887. The discovery of this inscription both proved that Burmese was used in the Bagan period and permitted the deciphering of the Pyu language, which had not been possible previously.

Modern Myanmar literature can be said to have had its beginnings in the 1930s when the University of Rangoon was founded and the Department of Myanmar Studies established. There was a new movement in literature known as the *Khitsan* movement whose writers used a simple and direct style that has continued to this day.

Present-day literature is still dominated by religious works, although there are many novels, short stories, poems, children's books, translations of foreign works, and works on culture, art, and science. Popular fiction consists mostly of romantic and *thaing* ("thai-ng") novels. Literary awards are presented annually. Many well-known writers are retired government servants, some of whom have worked or are working in institutes of higher learning. Most writers have a permanent job and write only in their spare time.

CRAFTS

In Myanmar, craftspeople and artisans are still able to make a living in spite of gradual industrialization. Among Myanmar's many crafts are silk and cotton weaving, lacquerware, gold and silverwork, wood and ivory carving, mosaics, tapestry-making, stone carving, boat-making, umbrella-making, and pottery.

The cotton and silk *longyi* that Myanmar men and women still wear, despite the growing popularity of Western dress among the young, are handwoven. Rakhine is famous for cotton woven *longyi* in the beautiful *acheik* ("er-CHAYK") design of twisted chains and spirals. Mandalay, Amarapura, and Pyi (or Pyay) are also famous for cotton woven fabrics, while Mudon, near Mawlamyine, is known for its cotton woven tablecloths and blankets. Fabric for silk *longyi* is woven in Mandalay and Amarapura and the Shan states. A favorite design is the beautiful multicolored *lun-ta-ya* ("loon-ter-yah"), or hundred shuttles. Other handwoven items include shawls and blankets from Pakokku in northwestern Myanmar and shoulder bags from Shan and Kachin, which are woven on a back-strap loom.

Tapestries, known as *kalagar* ("ker-lah-gah"), are popular tourist purchases and are made of appliqué designs on velvet or cotton cloth with glass beads and sequins stitched in. Traditional weaving designs include images of dancers, peacocks, elephants, and mythical animals.

Lacquerware is an ancient craft called *yun* ("YOON"), after the Yuns of north Thailand from whom the Myanmar learned the craft. Bagan and Pyi are lacquerware-producing areas. Typical articles are ashtrays, trinket boxes, vases, bowls, tables, and chests. The process involves coating a framework of woven bamboo with *thit-see* (raw lacquer obtained from a tree) and clay. The article is dried, after which several other coatings are applied. Finally, a design is hand-painted on the article.

A master woodcarver making wood puppets.

Gold leaf is regularly placed on the surface of pagodas as a form of worship. The gold-leaf industry is located in Mandalay. Gold is pounded until it is very thin, placed between thick bamboo paper, and packed for sale at pagodas. Golden ornaments set with gems are worn by Myanmar women and treated as a form of investment. There are goldsmiths in every town, where women come to sell and buy jewelry or have old jewelry reset in modern designs.

Silverware was once very popular. Myanmar women wore silver belts, and silver bowls were used by the well-to-do for weddings and festivals. But these articles are slowly becoming rare as family heirlooms, as their owners sell them to supplement incomes.

Pottery-making in Myanmar consists of plain earthenware for cooking pots, flowerpots, and water pots, and glazed ware for water jars, flower vases, pickle jars, and various small glazed articles such as ashtrays and pencil holders.

Left: **A Kayin (Karen) weaver.**

Below: **A lacquered *lepet* box.**

A craft related to religion is the making of Buddha images. Marble Buddha images are carved in Mandalay, while those cast in brass, copper, or silver Buddha images are made at Ywataung near Mandalay.

103

LEISURE

LEISURE TIME for the Myanmar people tends to be in the evening when the adults have returned from work and children have completed their homework.

GAMES

One game, the *htoke-see-htoe* ("TOHK-SEE-toh") is usually played on full-moon nights, and involves a lot of running and perspiration. Played with two teams, one team guards lines or rows that the other team tries to pass through.

Most Myanmar children have plenty of ingenuity and imagination: old, flat sardine cans are turned into cars by tying a string and pulling the can around, old bicycle tire rims are rolled along with a stick, and banana leaves and stems are made into toy guns, rings, and bracelets. Slingshots are easily made by carving a small piece of wood into a Y shape and tying a piece of rubber tubing to it. Pellets are made of mud from river banks, patiently rolled into small balls and dried in the sun.

Kites are flown in fields. The strings, rubbed with starch and glass powder, are so sharp that they can cut hands and even blind eyes. On a windy day, kites are flown with the main purpose of bringing down another kite by cutting it adrift.

On the tamer side, checkers can be played with bottle caps on cardboard boards. Grandparents teach their grandchildren to fold paper into ships, boats, animals, and other interesting objects. With so many kinds of games and playthings, there is almost no need for dolls and electronic toys.

Above: **Myanmar children are good at creating new games.**

Opposite: Enjoying a free ride on the ferris wheels at a festival in Mandalay. **These ferris wheels are hand-driven.**

SPORTS

Soccer is Myanmar's favorite and most popular sport. The spectators at national league soccer matches always fill the National Aung San stadium, often overflowing into the streets. During the 1960s and 1970s, Myanmar's national team was foremost in Southeast Asia, but in recent years it has sadly declined in performance. Soccer is played from boyhood with any kind of ball and is exciting to play and watch.

Chinlon, a traditional game once played to entertain the king, is a popular sport in Myanmar. It is played in proper courts and watched by many, or in the streets by young boys.

Chinlon is a traditional sport played with a cane ball made of rattan cane. It is hollow inside and about 16 inches (41 cm) in circumference. Usually, six players stand in a circle and try to keep the ball in the air using only their knees, heels, toes, elbows, shoulders, and head but not the hands. It is a simple game but requires great skill and good teamwork in tossing the ball around. *Chinlon* was once played to entertain the king, but it declined in popularity during the colonial period. In post-independence times, there have been great efforts to revive and promote it, and many *chinlon* associations have been formed. There are even women players who are so skilled that they can keep several cane balls going at once. A variation of *chinlon* is played like volleyball, over a net, with two teams participating.

Myanmar boxing is very violent even to most Myanmar spectators. The boxers are allowed to use any part of the body to fight, and the match is won by the person who draws first blood, which is actually fourth blood, as each boxer is allowed to wipe blood away three times before being declared the loser. A number of rules, such as trimmed nails and no kicking in the groin, scratching, or biting, have to be observed. The boxer's class is not determined by body weight, but by skill. A youngster begins in the lowest fourth class and moves up when he gets too good for his opponents in the same class. In matches, fighters are matched by weight and build within their own class. However, when a boxer reaches first class, he has to take on all opponents. Boxing matches, featuring famous boxers, travel from town to town and can be found at pagoda festivals. Boxing matches are accompanied by a Myanmar orchestra. Matches usually take place after the harvest until just before the rainy season.

Thaing is a Myanmar martial art and a form of self-defense. Players may use long swords called *dah* in one form of *thaing*. In recent years, it has been popularized in movies, comic strips, and novels featuring the heroes from the days of the kings.

In the villages, cockfighting is still found. It is a cruel sport since spurs are sharpened so as to hurt or kill the opponent. The spectators place bets.

Western sports such as tennis, golf, volleyball, basketball, and badminton are played in urban areas, but some sports like cricket, football, and baseball are not widely known. Rowing, yachting, table tennis, cycling, and hiking are also sports that have a number of enthusiasts in Yangon. Myanmar's track and field record in Southeast Asia has been outstanding, especially in the marathon.

Myanmar boxing is a violent sport in which the victor is the one who first draws blood.

STORYTELLING

Storytelling is common in the upbringing of children by all ethnic and social groups in Myanmar. Stories are told by grandparents, aunts, older sisters, and cousins to younger children to keep them quiet and to teach them good morals such as honesty, diligence, generosity, and faith. Most children love stories, and the favorite storyteller-aunts and cousins on a visit may be pestered until they give in and tell a story or two. There are many kinds of stories—folktales, ethnic tales, humorous tales, tales of kings, queens, princes, and princesses, and most important of all, the *Jataka* tales and the *Dhamma-pada*—tales from Buddha's life.

A grandmother telling a story to her grandchildren.

Folktales are handed down by word of mouth from generation to generation, and they tell of Master Golden Rabbit, Master Tiger, Master Fox, and some other animal's adventures that are funny and full of lessons to be learned. Master Simpleton, Mr. and Mrs. Deaf, and Mr. Clever are some of the typical characters of folktales.

Ethnic tales are told to preserve ethnic legends about the origin of the people of each group, their customs, and the meaning of the various festivals or celebrations. Humorous tales, some of which would not be mentioned in other societies, are accepted as natural and worthy of a hearty laugh. Tales of kings and life at court tell of heroes famous for qualities such as strength, courage, and perseverence in the face of danger and seemingly hopeless situations.

THE RABBIT'S COLD

Once upon a time a lion lived in a cave. His loyal subjects were the bear, the monkey, and the rabbit. One day the lion hit upon an idea to obtain food easily. First of all he called the bear to him, opened his mouth wide, and asked him what kind of smell he could smell. The bear said, "Oh Lion, I smell the smell of rotten meat." "What!" said the lion, "How dare you say that to me, the King of the Forest?" So saying, he bit the bear and ate him up.

Next he turned to the monkey and asked him the same question. Having seen what had happened to the honest bear, the monkey said, "Oh, Lion, your mouth has the fragrance of lilies." "What!" said the lion, "I who live on the meat of lesser animals cannot possibly have such fragrance issuing from my mouth! Do you dare to lie to me?" So the monkey went the same way as the bear.

Last was the rabbit's turn. The rabbit did not come up close to the lion, but said, "Oh, Lion, I have such a very bad cold, and my nose cannot detect any smell whatsoever. Allow me to go home and cure my cold first, please." With that, the rabbit ran away as fast as he could and never went near the lion's cave again.

FESTIVALS

The origin of the Myanmar calendar is not clear, but it was revised several times by different kings. It consists of 12 lunar months; 1361–1362 was equivalent to the Gregorian year 2000. The difference between the lunar year and the solar year is made up for by the addition of an extra month to the lunar calendar every few years. The Myanmar year begins in mid-April and ends in mid-March. Both the Myanmar and Gregorian calendars are widely used.

For religious matters, the Myanmar use the Buddhist calendar, which is also the lunar calendar, but the calculation begins from the year of Buddha's Enlightenment: 2000 was the year 2543–2544 on the Buddhist calendar.

THE MYANMAR CALENDAR

Myanmar months and corresponding English months:

Tagu	mid-March to mid-April
Kasone	mid-April to mid-May
Nayone	mid-May to mid-June
Waso	mid-June to mid-July
Wagaung	mid-July to mid-August
Tawthalin	mid-August to mid-September
Thadingyut	mid-September to mid-October
Tazaungmone	mid-October to mid-November
Nadaw	mid-November to mid-December
Pya-tho	mid-December to mid-January
Ta-bo-dwe	mid-January to mid-February
Tabaung	mid-February to mid-March

There is a festival for each month of the Myanmar calendar, beginning with the first month of Tagu.

Opposite: **Dancers at the Kachin Day festival.**

WATER FESTIVAL

The Water Festival, lasting four to five days, is celebrated in mid-April to welcome the Myanmar New Year. During this time, the Myanmar throw water on each other; the amount of water varies from a sprinkle of a few drops of perfumed water to bowls to bucketfuls. The festival symbolically washes away the old year's bad luck and sins, and it also serves the practical purpose of cooling off everyone when temperatures soar as high as 100°F (38°C) or more.

Special structures called *mandat* ("MUN-DART") are constructed at the side of main roads. These are usually open-sided shelters with bamboo poles supporting the bamboo-strip matting used for the roof. In front of the *mandat*, water barrels and pipes are lined up. During the festival, people participate either by throwing water at one of the *mandat* or by going from *mandat* to *mandat* in open jeeps, small trucks, or even large trucks or buses to have water thrown on them.

This water-throwing is for the young only. The elderly do not participate in the fun but go to monasteries or meditation centers for quiet meditation instead.

On the last day, New Year's Eve, no more water is thrown. The Myanmar welcome the New Year by setting free fish, birds, and cattle. The elderly have their hair washed by the younger people, who gain merit. Special feasts are given to the monks in the monasteries at this time.

BANYAN TREE-WATERING CEREMONY

In every pagoda and monastery in Myanmar, a banyan tree (*Ficus religiosa*) is planted because it was under the banyan tree that the Buddha attained Enlightenment. On the full moon night of Kasone, the second month of the Myanmar calendar, the banyan tree is watered by worshipers in a ceremony. This is a sacred day to the Buddhists, as it was on this day that the Buddha was born, later attained Enlightenment, and finally died. Worshipers, carrying earthen water pots, take turns watering the tree, whose base is enclosed in a decorative concrete structure.

At the banyan tree-watering ceremony, worshipers carrying earthen water pots take turns watering the tree in order to gain merit.

WASO ROBE-OFFERING CEREMONY (DHAMMA-SET-KYA DAY)

Dhamma-set-kya day, the full moon day of Waso, the fourth month in the Myanmar calendar, commemorates the preaching of the Buddha's first sermon 49 days after his Enlightenment. This day also marks the beginning of the Buddhist Lent, which lasts for the three months of the rainy season. The robe-offering ceremony is performed no later than the full-moon day of Waso, since during Lent the monks are required to spend the period at their monasteries and are forbidden to travel; the robes offered are for their use during this period of retreat.

For the people, Lent is a quiet time of restraint with few social activities; weddings are not celebrated, and most people do not move to a new home.

FESTIVAL OF LIGHTS

The festival of lights is celebrated at the end of Lent on the full-moon day of Thadingyut, which coincides with the end of the rainy season. This festival commemorates the descent of Buddha to Earth at the end of the three months of Lent when he preached to his divine mother the Buddhist Abidhamma, the most difficult of Buddhist teachings. Buddhist homes are lit up at night with paper lanterns hung on front porches or candles. Government offices and buildings are decorated with colorful electric lights. The festival lasts three days, from the eve of the full moon to the day after the full moon.

Faithful Buddhists cele-brating the Festival of Lights at the Shwe Dagon pagoda.

Since this festival marks the end of Lent, it is a time of great joy. Some streets are closed off at night and stages are erected at one end for all-night performances by dancers, comedians, singers, and musicians. Small stalls are set up, selling local foods and handicrafts.

It is the custom for young people to show their respect and gratitude to parents, teachers, and mentors by going to their homes with gifts of cakes, fruits, and other offerings. In making these offerings, the young people sit on the floor and make the gesture of obeisance three times, while the elders give blessings for good health, wealth, and safe passage through life.

KAHTEIN ROBE-OFFERING CEREMONY

The Kahtein robe-offering ceremony is performed during the month of Tazaungmone (mid-October to mid-November). Robes and other articles are offered to monks; feasts are also held, with many guests invited to take part in the merit-making.

A second festival of lights is held at this time, a month after the first festival of lights; again it lasts three days, from the eve of the full-moon day to the day after the full moon.

At Yangon's Shwe Dagon pagoda, an all-night weaving contest takes place where weavers spend the night weaving robes that must be completed at dawn when they are offered to the Buddha images at the pagoda. Other such all-night weaving takes place around the country.

On the night of the full moon, there is the custom of hiding other people's possessions in various places as a joke; for example, people might move the neighbors' flowerpots or water barrels, or remove the clothesline.

Worshipers praying at the Shwe Dagon pagoda.

HTA-MA-NE MAKING FESTIVAL

This festival celebrates the harvest and takes place in the month of Ta-bo-dwei. *Hta-ma-ne* ("ter-mah-NAIR") is made from glutinous rice, peanuts, ginger, oil, garlic, sesame seeds, and coconut. The ginger, garlic, and coconut are sliced thinly and added to the glutinous rice, and the mixture is cooked in large pans over open fires on monastery grounds or in private gardens. The mixture is so sticky that it has to be stirred by grown men with big wooden paddles. This rich and fragrant pudding is served to everyone.

115

HPAUNG-DAW-U FESTIVAL

In the month of Tawthalin, a unique pagoda festival, the *Hpaung-Daw-U* festival, takes place in Inle Lake in eastern Myanmar. Here, on and around Inle Lake, the Inthas live, weaving silk and cotton, fishing, and growing vegetables on floating gardens. They travel around in boats either rowed with oars or powered by outboard motors. The rowing is done in a standing position with one leg wrapped around the oar; hence, the Inthas are known as the "leg rowers of Inle Lake."

During this festival, three Buddha images from the pagoda are taken around on the lake in lovely decorated boats so that the people can worship from their own boats and homes as the images pass.

PAGODA FESTIVALS

Myanmar is a land of pagodas, and the more famous pagodas have their own festival days. The Shwe Dagon Pagoda festival is held around the full-moon day of Tabaung, the last month of the year.

Pagoda festivals have ferris wheels, all-night shows and dances, and stalls selling food, local handicrafts, and souvenirs. Villagers from all around attend, spending the night watching shows, eating favorite delicacies, and going home in their bullock carts in the morning.

ETHNIC FESTIVALS

Each of the ethnic groups in Myanmar has its own festivals. Of these, the better known ones are the Kayin New Year, the Kachin Manao festival, and the Pa-o rocket-firing festivals.

KAYIN NEW YEAR is celebrated on the new-moon day of the lunar month, Pya-tho, and is a national holiday. In Yangon, Karens gather at communal centers, and Don dances are performed by Karen girls and boys wearing the Karen dress. In Pa-an, capital of the Karen State, the Don is performed with great ceremony. Frog drums and buffalo horns are played.

KACHIN MANAO FESTIVAL The Kachins celebrate a victory or a prosperous period, or mark the illness or death of parents or the moving away of a family member with a *Manao* ("mer-NOW") festival.

The *Manao* involves great expense since there are many guests. Only chieftains (*duwa*) are capable of bearing the expense; one such festival involved the slaughtering of 14 buffaloes, 20 cows, 20 pigs, and 50 chickens, and 200 baskets of rice and 4,500 bottles of spirits. A large shelter, decorated with a huge pair of buffalo horns, is built with four *manao* poles in the center; drinking, eating, and dancing take place here.

PA-O ROCKET FESTIVAL This festival is celebrated by the Pa-o people who live in southern Shan State. During this festival, lengths of large bamboo poles or metal shells are filled with gunpowder, fuses are attached, and the "rockets" are fired from a 20 to 30-foot- (6 to 9-m) high rocket stand. This festival is celebrated from Tagu to Waso, the first four months of the Myanmar year, as an offering to the gods for a favorable climate, good harvest, and prosperous and peaceful new year.

FOOD

MYANMAR FOOD is not as well known as the other Asian cuisines of Thailand, China, India, or Japan.

Myanmar food consists primarily of different kinds of stewed dishes and curries. Side dishes include salads and stir-fried or boiled vegetables with delicious spicy dips.

KITCHENS

Myanmar kitchens are presided over by the female members of the household—the mother, elder daughters, aunts, or grandmothers.

In the kitchen, a low round table about one and a half feet (46 cm) in height is used, with low stools as seats. Common kitchen articles include a stone mortar and pestle, a chopping block—usually made of a round cross-section of a tree trunk—earthen or aluminum pots without handles, and earthen water jars. Wood or charcoal fires are used, since electricity and gas is available only in larger urban areas and kerosene is scarce.

Most of the kitchen activity takes place at floor level. Because the meat and vegetables are bought without benefit of storage or packaging, a lot of cleaning has to be done immediately after their purchase. For this, and for the cleaning of large pots, a corner of the kitchen usually has a water tap and water jars. Sometimes, washing is done outside the kitchen in the backyard where water is stored in large barrels of wood or metal.

Myanmar households use a "cat" safe, *kyaung-ein* ("chaung-ain"), to store cooked foods, leftovers, plates, forks and spoons, spices, and ingredients in bottles. The safe is a small wooden cupboard about four to five feet (122 to 152 cm) in height, a foot (30.5 cm) in depth, and two feet (61 cm) wide. The sides and front are made of wire mesh to give proper airing for the food inside; a couple of drawers provide space for cutlery.

Above: **A "cat safe."**

Opposite: **Chickens for sale on a street market in Yangon.**

119

MAIN INGREDIENTS

Rice is included in all meals and most snacks. It can be eaten as a salad, fried, cooked with coconut cream, or kneaded with fish. Rice is usually served with mild curries made with vegetables, chicken, fish, or seafood. Glutinous rice is steamed, boiled, or rolled in banana leaves with banana stuffing. Rice flour is used in many dishes, cakes, and desserts.

The Myanmar use many spices and herbs in their cooking, including fresh ones. Turmeric, chili, onions, garlic, and ginger are pounded in a stone mortar and cooked in oil before meat, fish, or vegetables are added. Coriander leaf, lemon grass, tamarind juice, fish sauce, and fish paste are used in many dishes.

Myanmar women cook without the help of written recipes. Recipes are handed down through generations by word of mouth, and one learns by doing rather than reading. However, Myanmar cookbooks have gained popularity in the last decade.

The Myanmar also eat Western bread, cakes, and cookies, but wheat flour and other baking ingredients are scarce, and Western cakes are only for special occasions. People give cakes to parents and elders on festival days as a sign of respect.

MEAT, VEGETABLES, AND FRUIT All kinds of meat are eaten by the Myanmar, but most people prefer fish, fish products, and shrimp. If meat is avoided, it is usually beef because the cow, used to plow the soil for rice, is regarded as a benefactor. Buddhists believe slaughtering a large animal for its meat is more sinful than killing a smaller one. Certain meats cannot be offered as food to monks including bear, elephant, snake, and tiger meat. Some monks are vegetarian, although there is no specific religious taboo on meat. Many laypeople avoid meat during the Buddhist Lenten months from July to October.

The Myanmar like to eat raw or blanched vegetables with fish sauce dips and to drink soups made from the freshly plucked tender leaves of certain tropical trees and shrubs. They enjoy eating the roselle leaf, a sour-tasting vegetable, and water greens, also known as the aquatic morning glory. Okra, drumstick-fruit (a vegetable), gourd (a large green fruit of the gourd vine), *chayote*, and eggplant are common vegetables. Backyard gardens provide fresh vegetables, and trees, in abundance even in and around the cities, provide fruit and tender leaves.

Because of the varied climate in the different regions of Myanmar, a wide variety of tropical and temperate vegetables and fruits is available. Many Myanmar plant their own vegetables and fruits.

Fruits such as strawberries, avocados, and oranges were introduced in the colonial period, while grapefruit and apples were introduced as late as the 1950s. Common local fruits are mango, durian, mangosteen, rambutan, tangerine, pear, watermelon, and jackfruit. Myanmar like to eat fruit peeled and cut to savor the taste of each individual piece.

Myanmar still use leaves to wrap food. Broad leaves such as banana leaf, *badan* leaf, and various palm leaves are used in the bazaar to wrap purchases of fish, meat, and vegetables. Banana leaves sometimes serve as plates at a feast. To enhance the flavor of traditional cakes, banana, bamboo, and palm leaves are used as wrappers when cooking; the juice of pandan leaves is used for its fragrance and green color.

121

BETEL BOX ("*KOON-IT*")

Betel-chewing is quite common among the Myanmar, and it is customary to offer monks betel for chewing in a lacquer betel box. Betel boxes come in tiers that have special small compartments in each tier for the required ingredients: betel leaves, betel nuts, white lime, and spices, and a metal betel-nut cutter.

Lacquer betel boxes come in many designs: red and green, gold and black, and an embossed gold and black design that is now very rare.

TRADITIONAL MYANMAR FARE

Since Myanmar lies between India and China, both Indian and Chinese influences can be found in the cuisine. Many Myanmar dishes are cooked in a Chinese manner, including stir-frying and using typical Chinese ingredients such as bean curd, bean sprouts, and soy sauce. Indian influence can be seen in the use of spices for curries. On special occasions, Myanmar serve *biryani* ("bee-ree-yan-ni"), an Indian dish of chicken cooked with spices and served with saffron rice.

A traditional Myanmar main meal consists of boiled rice, a soup, a salad, a curry of meat or fish, and vegetables eaten raw with fish-paste sauce, boiled, or fried. In rural areas, meat curries are only an occasional treat.

For breakfast, most Myanmar like to eat *mohinga* ("mo-HIN-GAH"), rice noodles in a fish soup. Certain towns in Myanmar are famous for different types of *mohinga*. Steamed glutinous rice with toasted dried fish, sesame powder, and grated coconut is also a favorite. Another breakfast favorite is *nan-piah* ("nan-PIAH"), a flat Indian wheat bread, eaten with boiled beans tossed in an oil and salt dressing. Fried rice made from leftover rice from the previous evening also makes an adequate breakfast. Bread is eaten only in the main urban areas, and even then, only occasionally.

Below: Lepet is pickled tea leaves eaten as a savory snack with dried shrimps, peanuts, sesame seeds, fried garlic, and fried beans with an oil and salt dressing. The pickled tea leaves are first marinated in oil and pounded garlic. With *lepet*, one usually drinks plain tea. This snack is served to visitors at feasts and in homes. Older people like to eat just plain *lepet*, which is believed to have medicinal properties.

SNACKS, SALADS, AND DESSERTS Many Myanmar enjoy eating fried snacks, which are usually fritters of onions, beans, bananas, or gourd. Myanmar salads are made of raw or boiled vegetables, or meat mixed with sliced onion, garlic, dried shrimp powder, ground peanuts, roasted bean powder, fish sauce, lime or tamarind juice, and oil (which is cooked with turmeric to remove the oily taste).

Dessert may be fruit, peeled and cut to retain its natural taste, fruit preserves, nuts, or jaggery (palm sugar balls) served with plain tea. Traditional desserts are made from coconut, rice, or glutinous rice flour, and jaggery. Coconut cream is an essential ingredient in traditional Myanmar desserts. Many desserts have fancy names such as "golden heart cooler," "butterfly," and "smooth as marble."

DRINKS

Alcohol is avoided by most Myanmar who are devout Buddhists, except perhaps for rare social occasions and in the urban areas. The drinking of alcohol in any form is generally regarded as an indication of poor morals and constitutes a violation of basic Buddhist precepts. However, a traditional wine made from toddy palm or *dani* ("der-NI") (a palm that grows in swamps) is drunk by those in rural areas as a pastime or at festivals.

The only drink at the end of a meal is water or Myanmar tea. Coffee or tea is drunk at breakfast or sometimes at tea time, in a ready-mix brew with condensed milk. Soft drinks, known as aerated water in Myanmar, are served on special occasions.

ROADSIDE WATER-POT STAND

The gift of water holds special significance for Buddhists who believe it brings 10 merits: longevity, beauty, riches, strength, knowledge, cleanliness, fame, friends, never being in need of water, and being as swift as flowing water.

Buddhists offer water to the Buddha in household shrines, dig wells, and build water-pot stands for thirsty travelers in order to gain religious merit. These small stands are four-legged and made of wood, with a roof to give cover to the pots and cups. The base around the pot is sometimes filled with sand to keep the water cool, and bright green rice seedlings are grown in the sand to lighten the heart of the weary.

Alcoholic drinks are sold freely in Myanmar. However, the Myanmar people mostly practice temperance, and there are no drinking customs as such among the Myanmar. Social drinking is mostly found among Western-educated Myanmar. Generally, drinking is associated with alcoholism.

Ethnic Burmans drink toddy wine or *dani* wine, while most of the other ethnic groups drink wine made from rice or glutinous rice. A low quality home brew called country spirits, or "CS," is made from rice or corn and is available all over the country.

Among the ethnic groups, the Chin people who live in the western mountains drink a sweet wine, *khaung yei* ("kaong-yay"). They have the custom of drinking wine with a friend from the same container, usually a bamboo section. *Hlaw sa* ("hlor-zah"), the fermented rice from which *khaung yei* is extracted, can be eaten as a kind of pudding.

A bamboo container and cup used for drinking water or alcohol.

Many ethnic groups celebrate festivities with drinking. At the Kachin Manao Festival, it is said that up to 3,000 bottles of *khaung yei* and 1,500 bottles of country spirits are needed for the numerous guests. The Pa-o people living in the Shan State also drink in celebration before the rocket-firing festival. Ethnic Karens drink at funerals and at bone-collecting ceremonies.

MEALTIMES

Mealtimes in Myanmar are generally earlier than Western mealtimes. In rural areas, the family wakes before dawn, at about 4 A.M., and breakfast is at about 5 or 6 A.M. In the urban areas, breakfast is at about 7 A.M. The midday meal is taken at about noon; office workers carry their own food to the office in a small lunch box or tiered lunch carrier. In place of afternoon tea, a main meal is served at about 5 P.M. In urban areas where there is little or no night life, a light snack with a pot of Myanmar tea might be sufficient for supper at 10 or 11 P.M. Bedtime is even earlier in villages due to the lack of electricity and other lighting fuel.

A Myanmar family sits down to a meal. The Myanmar prefer to eat with their fingers.

TABLE MANNERS

The Myanmar do not dine in the Western sense of savoring food or wines and making conversation. The meal is quickly eaten and is over when one is full. There is no lingering at the dinner table, and guests may leave quite soon after eating. Dishes are full of flavor, but there is no emphasis on decoration or garnish. A meal does not consist of different courses. Instead, the dishes are placed in the center of the kitchen table, usually a low round table, with the diners seated on low stools as seats. In urban houses, there are Western-type dining tables and chairs. There is no specific seating arrangement. Portions from all the dishes are placed on one's plate and eaten with rice.

The most important eating etiquette is to serve the head of the family or oldest member first. Even if this person is not present at the time, it is customary to reserve the first portion for him or her. If fingers are used, and many Myanmar feel that eating this way is more conducive to hearty enjoyment of the meal, then the fingers must be washed first.

Generally, there is not much conversation during the meal. Talking with one's mouth full, talking about topics such as body wastes, and making noises are inappropriate and must be avoided at all costs. Eating too slowly, lying down or slouching, and sighing are regarded as being disrespectful at the meal table.

If there are guests, they should be pressed to have some more food, and even if they say no, their host may insist on serving them another portion. This is part of the Myanmar hospitality.

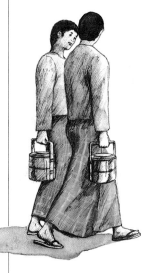

Office workers carry their lunches to work in tiered tiffin carriers.

SAGO DESSERT

1 cup of pearl sago, washed and drained
2 cups of palm water (jaggery)
3 cups of water

1 tbsp butter or margarine
2 cups of grated coconut
A pinch of salt

METHOD
Grease a tray with butter.
Boil 1 cup of water in a saucepan with palm sugar until the sugar is dissolved. Strain the liquid and set it aside.
Boil sago with 2 cups of water until the sago is transparent.
Add in palm sugar syrup and simmer the mixture over a low fire for 5 minutes.
Pour mixture into the greased tray and cool until the mixture is set.
Add a pinch of salt to the grated coconut. When the sago has cooled, scoop out spoonfuls of sago and roll them in the grated coconut.

When a feast is being held, relatives pitch in to help with the cooking and food preparation.

FEASTS

A Myanmar feast usually involves an offering of food and other items to monks, with guests arriving later to join in. Such feasts may take place in one's own home or at a monastery. The number of guests varies from a few close relatives to hundreds arriving at staggered intervals throughout the day. The occasion for a feast may be a birthday, a novitiation, an ear-piercing ceremony, a christening, or a wedding anniversary. It could be to gain merit for one's deceased parents or for oneself by donating toward building a new monastery, or offering robes on festival days.

The most sumptuous dishes are served at these feasts. The wealthier the host, the greater the variety of dishes served. Pork, chicken, seafood, *hilsa* (a kind of fish), and butterfish are made into curries, and it is important that they be cooked to perfection. Many side dishes of salads and delicious desserts are also served.

If the feast is held in the home, close relatives may sometimes bring their offerings of food for the monks. The night before the feast is one of great activity. The living room has to be cleared of chairs and tables, and carpets or smooth mats laid out. Special places are set aside for the monks. If the food to be offered is cooked at home, a small army of cooks composed of relatives—with a repertoire of tasty dishes—and a number of volunteer helpers may be seen peeling and cleaning the onions, garlic, and ginger. The food to be cooked

At most Myanmar feasts, offerings of robes and presents are made to monks who are then invited to a meal *(below)*. After this, the other guests are served *(left)*.

will have been bought on several marketing trips days before. The food is cooked during the night; the pots are so big that a fire using firewood has to be built outside in the backyard. In the villages, all the villagers or neighbors may come to help or at least give support by their presence. If the feast is held in a monastery, it is customary to order the food or have it cooked on the grounds by staff from the monastery.

When the monks arrive, they are offered the food, after which a suitable sermon is delivered and certain *sutras* ("SOOT-tras") chanted to bestow on the audience protection from danger, illness, and misfortune. Then the host and hostess share their merit with all beings, and guests praise the merit by saying *sadhu* ("sah-DOO," meaning well-done) three times. Then the guests are served food.

BURMESE PRAWN CURRY

1 cup oil
.1 teaspoon turmeric
1/2 teaspoon chilli powder
1 cup onion, sliced or pounded
1 clove garlic, sliced or pounded
1 or 2 tomatoes, diced
10 to 12 prawns, shelled and deveined
1 tablespoon fish sauce
1 or 2 sprigs of cilantro,
cut finely

Heat oil, put in turmeric, chilli powder, onion, and garlic and fry till fragrant and dry. Add tomatoes and continue frying till tomatoes are soft. Add prawns and cook till the prawns turn pink. Slowly add the fish sauce over the prawns and stir lightly. Sprinkle the coriander over the prawns, and turn off the fire when the coriander is lightly cooked but still green. Serve with white rice and a green salad.

HTAMANE

1 cup vegetable oil
1-inch piece of fresh ginger, cut into thin strips
1 cup glutinous rice (wash and soak in water overnight)
1 cup coconut milk, mixed with 1 tsp sugar
water enough to come up to 1 inch above the rice (in the pan)
1 cup peanuts, roasted and skinned
1 cup sesame seeds, roasted
1 cup cashew nuts, roasted and lightly crushed (optional)
1 cup pistachio nuts, roasted and lightly crushed (optional)
3 cloves garlic, thinly sliced
1 1/2 tsp salt
hot water

Use a medium-sized wok, put in oil and heat till hot. Add ginger strips and fry till fragrant and light brown. Add glutinous rice and stir till well-coated with ginger oil. Next put in water and coconut milk and stir till mixed. Cover and cook over low fire till the rice is cooked and very soft; add hot water, a little at a time, and keep stirring till rice grains become mushy. Add peanuts, sesame seeds, cashew nuts and pistachios, and continue stirring till well-blended. Sprinkle salt and stir. *Htamane* is done when the oil is on top and all the water is absorbed. The mixture must be sticky and mushy.

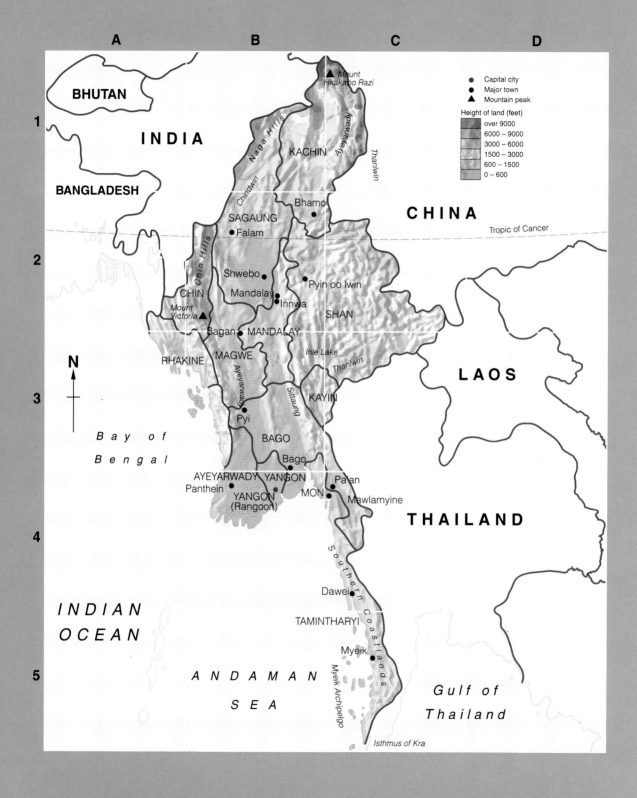

BHUTAN

INDIA

BANGLADESH

▲ Mount Hkakabo Razi

KACHIN

Naga Hills

Chindwin

Mali

Thanlwin

Bhamo

CHINA

Tropic of Cancer

SAGAUNG

Falam

Chin Hills

Shwebo

Pyin oo lwin

CHIN

Mandalay

Innwa

SHAN

Mount Victoria ▲

Bagan

MANDALAY

RHAKINE

MAGWE

Inle Lake

Thanlwin

Ayeyarwady

Sittaung

KAYIN

Pyi

Bay of Bengal

BAGO

Bago

AYEYARWADY YANGON

Pathein

Pa'an

MON

Mawlamyine

YANGON (Rangoon)

THAILAND

LAOS

N

Capital city
Major town
▲ Mountain peak

Height of land (feet)
over 9000
6000 – 9000
3000 – 6000
1500 – 3000
600 – 1500
0 – 600

INDIAN OCEAN

Southern Coastlands

Dawei

TAMINTHARYI

Myeik

ANDAMAN SEA

Myeik Archipelgo

Gulf of Thailand

Isthmus of Kra

A   B   C   D

1
2
3
4
5

MAP OF MYANMAR

Andaman Sea, B5

Ayeyarwady (state), B4

Ayeyarwady River, C1–C3

Bagan, B2

Bago (state), B3

Bago (town), B3

Bangladesh, A1

Bengal, Bay of, A3

Bhamo, B2

Bhutan, A1

Chin, A2–B2

Chin Hills, B2

China, C1–D1

Chindwin River, B1, B2

Dawei, C4

Falam, B2

Gulf of Thailand, C5–D5

India, A1–B1

Indian Ocean, A4–A5

Inle Lake, B3–C3

Innwa, B2

Isthmus of Kra, B5, C5

Kachin, B1

Kayin (Karen), B3–C3

Laos, C3–D3

Magwe, B3

Mandalay (state), B2–B3

Mandalay (town), B2

Mawlamyine, C4

Mon, C4

Mount Hkakabo Razi, B1

Mount Victoria, B2

Myeik, C5

Myeik Archipelago, C5

Naga Hills, B1

Pa'an, C4

Pathein, B3

Pegu (town), B3

Pegu (state), B3

Pyi, B3

Pyin oo lwin (Maymyo), B2

Rakhine, A3–B3

Sagaung, B2

Shan, C2

Shwebo, B2

Sittaung River, B3

Southern coastlands, C4–C5

Tanintharyi, C4

Thailand, C4–D4

Thanlwin River, C1–C3

Yangon (state), B3

Yangon (town), B3

ECONOMIC MYANMAR

KACHIN

SAGAUNG

CHIN

RHAKINE

MANDALAY

SHAN

MAGWE

KAYIN

BAGO

AYEYARWADY

YANGON

MON

TAMINTHARYI

Manufacturing

 Antiques

 Tapestries

 Textiles

 Brassware and Copperware

 Lacquer Ware

Natural Resources

 Jade

 Ruby

 Sapphires

 Emeralds

 Fish and Fish Products

 Shrimp and Shrimp Products

 Oil and Gas

 Tin

Agriculture

 Wheat

 Rice

 Beans

 Rubber

 Tobacco

 Tropical Fruits

 Temperate Fruits

 Coconut and Coconut Products

Cultured Pearls

ABOUT
THE ECONOMY

OVERVIEW
Myanmar's GDP structure remains the same as it has for decades: agriculture 47 percent, industries 11 percent, services 42 percent

POPULATION
49.13 million (1999)

GROSS DOMESTIC PRODUCT
US$59.4 billion (1999)

GDP GROWTH
4.6%

LAND USE
25 million acres [hectares] (net sown area; 1999)

AGRICULTURAL PRODUCTS
Rice, beans, and peas

MINERAL RESOURCES
Oil and gas, gems, metals

INFLATION RATE
25 percent (2000)

TOTAL EXPORTS
US$1.2 billion (1998)

MAJOR EXPORTS
Teak, beans, peas, prawns

TOTAL IMPORTS
US$2.5 billion (1998)

MAJOR IMPORTS
Machineries and metals

MAIN TRADING PARTNERS
Singapore, Thailand, China, India, Malaysia, Japan

EXTERNAL DEBT
US$5.4 billion

WORKFORCE
Age:15–59 years
Working population: 29.1 million (1999)

UNEMPLOYMENT RATE
3–4 percent (1999)

HIGHWAYS
18,299 miles/29,443 km (1999)

RAILROADS
3,789 miles/6,097 km (1999)

CURRENCY
Kyats (Ks) and pyas; 100 pyas=Ks 1.
US$1=Ks 6
Currency notes in denominations of Ks 1, 5, 10, 15, 45, 50, 90,100, 200, 500, 1000. Coins not in use.

CULTURAL MYANMAR

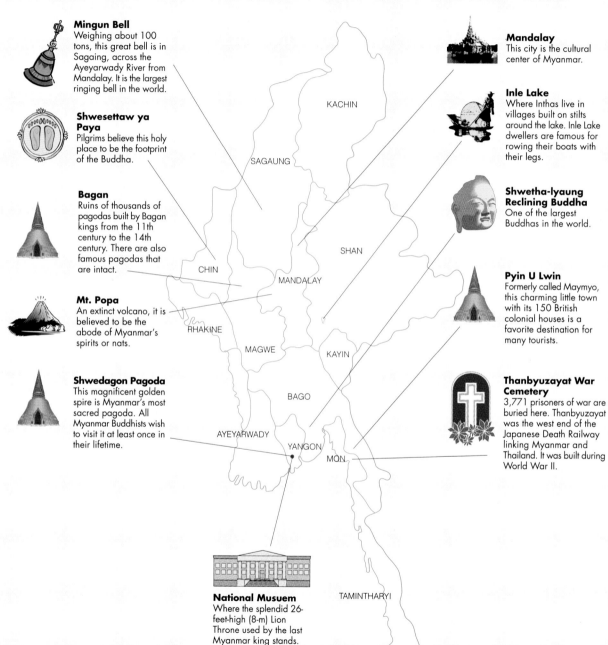

Mingun Bell
Weighing about 100 tons, this great bell is in Sagaing, across the Ayeyarwady River from Mandalay. It is the largest ringing bell in the world.

Shwesettaw ya Paya
Pilgrims believe this holy place to be the footprint of the Buddha.

Bagan
Ruins of thousands of pagodas built by Bagan kings from the 11th century to the 14th century. There are also famous pagodas that are intact.

Mt. Popa
An extinct volcano, it is believed to be the abode of Myanmar's spirits or nats.

Shwedagon Pagoda
This magnificent golden spire is Myanmar's most sacred pagoda. All Myanmar Buddhists wish to visit it at least once in their lifetime.

Mandalay
This city is the cultural center of Myanmar.

Inle Lake
Where Inthas live in villages built on stilts around the lake. Inle Lake dwellers are famous for rowing their boats with their legs.

Shwetha-lyaung Reclining Buddha
One of the largest Buddhas in the world.

Pyin U Lwin
Formerly called Maymyo, this charming little town with its 150 British colonial houses is a favorite destination for many tourists.

Thanbyuzayat War Cemetery
3,771 prisoners of war are buried here. Thanbyuzayat was the west end of the Japanese Death Railway linking Myanmar and Thailand. It was built during World War II.

National Musuem
Where the splendid 26-feet-high (8-m) Lion Throne used by the last Myanmar king stands.

KACHIN

SAGAUNG

CHIN

MANDALAY

RHAKINE

MAGWE

SHAN

KAYIN

BAGO

AYEYARWADY

YANGON

MON

TAMINTHARYI

ABOUT
THE CULTURE

OFFICIAL NAME
Union Of Myanmar

FLAG DESCRIPTION
Red with a blue rectangle in the upper hoist-side corner with 14 five-pointed, white stars surrounding a cogwheel which contains a stalk of rice; the 14 stars represent the 14 administrative divisions.

LAND AREA
261,228 square miles (67,658 square km)

CAPITAL
Rangoon, renamed Yangon in June 1989

AGE STRUCTURE
0-14 years: 30%
(male 6,341,546; female 6,086,650)
15-64 years: 65%
(male 13,565,379; female 13,764,242)
65 years and over: 5%
(male 885,583; female 1,091,453) (2000 est.)

POPULATION GROWTH RATE
0.64% (2000 est.)

BIRTH RATE
20.61 births/1,000 population (2000 est.)

DEATH RATE
12.35 deaths/1,000 population (2000 est.)

ETHNIC GROUPS
Bamar 68%, Shan 9%, Karen 7%, Rakhine 4%, Chinese 3%, Mon 2%, Indian 2%, other 5%

RELIGIONS
Buddhist 89%, Christian 4% (Baptist 3%, Roman Catholic 1%), Muslim 4%, animist 1%, other 2%

LANGUAGES
Burmese, minority ethnic groups have their own languages

LITERACY
83.1% of population age 15 and above

IMPORTANT ANNIVERSARIES
Independence Day, January 4, celebrates the day indepedence was declared in 1948.
Union Day, February 12, commemorates the signing of the Pang-long Agreement in 1947.
Armed Forces Day, March 7, celebrates the defeat of the Japanese in 1947.
National Day, 26th of the lunar month of Tazaungmon, commemorates the 1920 strike by university students against the British government.

LEADERS IN POLITICS
General Ne Win: former Chairman of the previous BSPP and President of Myanmar
General Aung San: Father of Burma's independence
Daw Aung San Suu Kyi: General Secretary, National League for Democracy

TIME LINE

IN MYANMAR	IN THE WORLD
	753 B.C. Rome founded
	116–17 B.C. Roman Empire reaches its greatest extent, under Emperor Trajan (98–17 B.C.).
	A.D. 600 Height of Mayan civilization
	1000 Chinese perfect gunpowder and begin to use it in warfare.
A.D. 1057 King Anawrahta defeats the Mons and unifies the country under the First Myanmar Empire.	
1084 King Kyanzittha, Anawratha's son, is elected to the throne. The golden age of pagoda-building at Bagan begins.	
1287 The Mongols, under Kublai Khan, conquer Bagan and the last Myanmar empire falls.	
	1530 Beginning of trans-Atlantic slave trade organized by Portuguese in Africa
1558 King Bayinnaung, Tabinshwehti's successor, founds the Second Myanmar Empire.	**1558–1603** Reign of Elizabeth I of England
	1620 Pilgrim Fathers sail the Mayflower to America
1755 King Alaungpaya founds the Third Myanmar Empire at Shwebo, north of present-day Mandalay.	**1776** U. S. Declaration of Independence
	1789–1799 The French Revolution
1824 The first Anglo-Myanmar war breaks out. Burma is defeated.	
1852 Second Anglo-Myanmar war. The British take control of Lower Burma.	**1861** U. S. Civil War begins.
1885 Third Anglo-Myanmar war led by King Thibaw, who is exiled to India and Burma is ruled as part of British India.	**1869** The Suez Canal is opened.

IN MYANMAR	IN THE WORLD
	1914 World War I begins.
1937 Burma is separated from India and has a new constitution and its own legislative council.	**1939** World War II begins.
1945 The Japanese surrender in August.	**1945** The United States drops atomic bombs on Hiroshima and Nagasaki.
1948 Burma gains independence. U Nu becomes Prime Minister.	**1949** North Atlantic Treaty Organization (NATO) formed
	1957 Russians launch Sputnik.
1962 General Ne Win comes into power following a military coup, and Burma isolates itself.	**1966–1969** Chinese Cultural Revolution
1974 The Socialist Republic of the Union of Burma is created.	**1986** Nuclear power disaster at Chernobyl in Ukraine
1988 The military government declares that Burma is no longer on a socialist path.	
1989 Burma is renamed Union of Myanmar.	
1989 Daw Aung San Suu Kyi, leader of the opposition party, the National League for Democracy, is placed under house arrest. Released in 1995.	
1990 Elections held for the first time in 30 years.	**1991** Break-up of Soviet Union
1997 Myanmar joins ASEAN. SLORC changes its name to State Peace and Development Council.	**1997** Hong Kong is returned to China.
2000 Myanmar comes under increasing fire from international organizations such as the United Nations and the International Labour Organization (ILO) for human rights abuses.	**2001** World population surpasses 6 billion.

GLOSSARY

aingyi ("AYN-jee")
Myanmar blouse or shirt.

biryani ("bee-ree-ya-nee")
Indian rice dish with chicken and spices.

coup d'etat
The violent overthrow of an existing government.

Daw
Honorific for adult female.

Dhamma ("der-mah")
Teachings of the Buddha, also spelt "Dharma."

jaggery
Palm sugar balls eaten as a dessert with plain tea.

Jataka ("jah-ter-kah")
Tales from Buddha's life.

kadawt ("ker-DORHT")
Gesture of homage or obeisance.

koon-it ("KOON-it")
Betel box for putting in the ingredients for chewing betel.

mandat ("MAHN-dat")
A marquee-like structure made of bamboo matting and bamboo poles.

merit
To better one's life in this and future existences, one has to gain merit through performances of good deeds, such as giving alms to the monks.

mohinga ("mo-HIN-GAH")
Rice noodles in fish soup, eaten at breakfast.

nat ("nah-t")
Spirit.

pandan ("PAHN-dan")
Screwpine plant whose leaves are used for their flavor and to obtain green color in cakes and other desserts.

sadhu ("SAR-doo")
Pali word meaning "well done," repeated three times after a Buddhist ceremony.

saya
Honorific for teacher or elder.

thanaka ("tha-ner-KAH")
Pale yellow paste applied to face and arms of women to protext their skin and keep cool.

U
Honorific for male adult.

ZAT ("ZAHT")
Traditional Myanmar drama.

FURTHER INFORMATION

BOOKS

Clark, Michael and Joe Cummings. *Lonely Planet Myanmar*. 7th ed. London: Lonely Planet Publications, 1999.

Courtauld, Caroline and Martin Morland. *Burma (Myanmar)*. 2nd ed. New York: Odyssey Publications, 1998.

Froese, Deborah and Wang Kui (illustrator). *The Wise Washerman: A Folktale from Burma*. New York: Disney Press, 1996.

Khng, Pauline. *Countries of the World: Myanmar*. Singapore: Times Editions, 2000.

Ling, Bettina and Charlotte Bunch. *Aung San Suu Kyi: Standing Up for Democracy in Burma (Women Changing the World)*. New York: Feminist Press, 1999.

Wright, David K. *Burma: Enchantment of the World*. Dublin: Children's Press, 1996.

Yip, Dora and Pauline Khng. *Welcome to Myanmar*. Singapore: Times Editions, 2001.

WEBSITES

Central Intelligence Agency World Factbook (select Burma from the country list). www.odci.gov/cia/publications/factbook/index.html

Learning Network reference (type "Myanmar" in the search box). http://ln.infoplease.com

Lonely Planet World Guide: Destination Myanmar. www.lonelyplanet.com/destinations/south_east_asia/myanmar

The Myanmar government. www.myanmar.com

The New Light of Myanmar, a daily newspaper. www.myanmar.com/nlm

The World Bank Group (type "Myanmar" in the search box). www.worldbank.org

U.S. Department of State: Burma Country Report on Human Rights Practices for 1998. www.state.gov/www/global/human_rights/1998_hrp_report/burma.html

VIDEOS

Raising the Bamboo Curtain: Awakening Burma/Cambodia and Vietnam. Narrated by Martin Sheen. Released 1994.

BIBLIOGRAPHY

Aung Aung Taik. *Under the Golden Pagoda: The Best of Burmese Cooking.* San Francisco: Chronicle Books, 1993.

Aung San Suu Kyi. *Burma: Let's Visit Places and Peoples* (Illustrated). London: Chelsea House, 1988.

Aung San Suu Kyi. *Freedom From Fear and other Writings.* Penguin Books, 1991.

Houghton, Graham and Wakefield, Julie. *Burma.* London: Macmillan's Children Books, 1988.

The Voice of Hope: Conversations with Alan Clements. Penguin Books, 1997.

Movies (Video):

Beyond Rangoon (1995) starring Patricia Arquette: Plot woven around the 1988 uprising in Myanmar. Filmed in Penang, Malaysia.

INDEX